Transformational Thinking

The First Step toward Achieving Personal and Organizational Greatness

Dr. Terence Jackson

Dedicated to all who want to transform the world

You must THINK differently

You cannot apply old frameworks to new problems

ISBN-13: 978-1548487676

ISBN-10: 1548487678

Table of Contents

Thought (Thinking) is the only true business of life.

You are at all times dealing with magical power of thought and consciousness.

What results can you expect so long as you remain oblivious to the power which can be within your control ?

Change versus Transformation. Change is essentially a comparison to something that previously existed. By its very nature, change is past-based. Essentially, change yields more, better, or different from what came before. Transformation, on the other hand, is an act of bringing forth or inventing. It is something created, and is inherently expansive and infinite. Are you changing or Transforming?

INTRODUCTION

Traditional Thinking (What Has It Produced)

We are living in tumultuous times. The global financial markets are near collapse. Our educational system is committing what a friend of mine, Dr. Clarence Thomas III, would call capital crimes (capital crimes are punishable by death) because they do not teach students how to think, how to learn, how to read, how to write, or to do arithmetic. Our social systems are bursting at the seams as we have millions seeking assistance from the government due to our poor educational system and lack of job creation within our economy. Corporations are having massive layoffs. Unemployment is skyrocketing. We have parents who cannot control or discipline their children. Better yet, they have become afraid of their children. The religious institutions are taking the people's money and not helping the church members when they need it. The ministers are being caught up in thinking they are GOD when they should be serving the members of the church. Our justice system is burdened with more inmates than it can hold because we have not discovered the root causes for why criminals commit crimes in hopes that we can reduce or prevent crimes from happening. The justice system has also targeted certain groups of people to incarcerate. Our politicians for the most part, only look out for their best interest. They deal in corruption; lie to their constituents, and think they are above the law because they make the law. They get richer as their constituents become poorer. Politicians do not want to be held accountable. Have you stopped to think why we are here? Have you asked "what is it about how we think that has created these turbulent times" or do you even think? If you think, do you think for yourself or does someone (or the system) think for you. Have you ever asked yourself "why do I think as I do?"

We are where we are because of how we think. Our best thinking has brought us here today. We all have been conditioned to think the same way. We train animals to be obedient and train human beings to do the same. The concepts we teach in school do not lend themselves to thinking differently.

Television reinforces what we are taught in school as well as reinforcing how we should think based on societal expectations of our thoughts. We often refer to the concept of "thinking out of the box" however, we are not taught to think out of the box. The box has been created for us by all of the theories that we have been taught to subscribe to as learners. Is it possible to "think out of the box?" Let's examine this concept.

Thinking out of the Box is an often used phrase through society. Out of the box thinking is defined as "thinking that moves away in diverging directions so as to involve a variety of aspects and which sometimes lead to novel ideas and solutions; associated with creativity." From childhood we are taught what to do by our parents, teachers, ministers, and other social institutions. As a result, we are not taught to think out of the box. A box is built around us that provide us with points of reference (theories and thought processes). Reflect back to your math, chemistry, physics, accounting, finance and English courses. Do you remember the formulas that you were asked to memorize? Do you remember from you history class the information that you were asked to memorize? Would you say that the box in which you live was created by those learning's? Now, think about what you learned in church and how that impacts how you think. Would you agree that you box has been created for you? In all of these learning's would you say that you have also been taught how to "think out of the box?" The masses have not been taught how to think out of the box and this way of thinking is known as Traditional Thinking.

Traditional Thinking, our best thinking, has us where we are today. It has produced the country and citizens that we are today. Our greatness and our shortcomings are a result of Traditional Thinking. Our current reality is a product of that thinking and the choices made with options that were available at the time. Albert Einstein said the level of thought that was used to create the problem cannot not be the same level of thought that provides a solution to the problem. Traditional Thinking has produced a country that no longer reports the results of how are students place against other countries in math and science competitions. Why have we ceased reporting such results, because Traditional Thinking does not enable us to teach our students what they need to compete in the global society? If we do not shed Traditional Thinking and embrace Transformational Thinking we will become a third world country.

TRANSFORMATIONAL THINKING: A PHILOSOPHY

Thought is the precursor to what was, what is, and what will be. When we transform our thoughts we transform the kind of decisions we make, the kind of actions we take, and ultimately we transform the results we produce. This is why we must transform our thinking. We must produce better results than we have in the past.

Transformational Thinking is a philosophy that teaches one to challenging all assumptions. Throughout history every great leader has become great because they challenged the assumptions of their time and transformed society. Their thinking was different from the masses of the people. Reflect on leaders such as Jesus, Gandhi, King, Malcolm, Buffet, Gates, President Barack Obama and Mandela. Monumental shifts occurred as a result of their ability to transform their thinking and the thinking of the masses.

Transformational Thinking isn't intended to be a 'stand-alone' philosophy. It isn't Communism, Capitalism, Buddhism, Catholicism, Corporatism or any other 'ism' out there. It is a framework into which any other belief can fit. What it does promise to be is a reality improvement tool and the only reality you will ever need to improve is your own.

I believe that there is much to be done in this world if we are to proactively make it what it should be. Our best thinkers got the world to the state it is in today, just as your best thinking got you to where you are today. Wherever that may be in the great scheme of things, we could all use a little improvement, some more than most. This is where Transformational Thinking comes in.

The concept of Transformational Thinking is a collection of tools that have been used in a variety of different roles by some of the world's most respected thinkers. Alongside these and into the framework of the concept, I have humbly placed my own. By bringing together some very useful skills and harnessing the power that has been scattered across the thinking spectrum, Transformational Thinking has emerged.

In a different arena, when we observe great athletes and coaches, there are those that stand out from the rest. When we study the likes of Michael Jordan, Tiger Woods, Phil Jackson, Deion Sanders, Tom Brady, Vince Lombardi, Muhammad Ali, Bill Belichick, Lebron James, Usain Bolt, Michael Phelps, Gabby Douglas and Chuck Noll we ask what separates these individuals from their peers. What drove their successes? What differentiated them from other athletes and coaches that have played or coached their respective sports? Many would argue that it was how they think that differentiated them from their peers. In the book "Overachievement: The New Science of Working Less to Achieve More" John Eliot, Ph.D. posits that top performers in every field think differently when all the marbles are on the line. In other words these top performs transformed their thinking in such a way that they reached higher levels of performance than their peers. Not only do top performers think differently but they also teach their colleagues to think differently.

TRANSFORMATIONAL THINKING: A CALL TO ARMS

This is a call to arms. It is about finding and implementing solutions, not placing blame and shame for the problems. It is a movement that must begin deep within each of us. We must transform our own beliefs and thinking in order to solve the problems that we, not "they", have created. It is time to expand the parameters of our own perception, to tap into the personal power we all possess and only then, individually and collectively, can we successfully increase the quality of our reality, creating an environment that is conducive for sustainable personal and collective growth.

I believe we can do it. I believe the problem is not as vast and complicated as we would like to believe. I maintain that we can and must solve the problems within our own homes, neighborhoods and society as a whole, starting with that which is the product of our very lives. *We can change the world*, provided we are *willing to change ourselves*.

That is the purpose of this book. It is not descriptive in approach. We all know what the problems are. It is prescriptive. It contains the skills and tools we need to accomplish the task that is our responsibility as adults, parents, teachers and children. It is an approach that is broad and respectful enough to include all people in all of our societies, whatever their age, whatever their religion, whatever their creed or belief system might be. Each of us has contributed to the current reality of our world and there is much that every single individual within it can contribute toward a sustainable improvement, provided there is a general approach of mutual respect and trust.

Although each of our societies on Earth have differing values and attitudes, it is time for us all to divert our energy, intelligence and creativity from activities of violence and destruction and redirect it towards building societies and cultures that provide the love and respect we are all looking for, and so richly deserve.

This should serve as *your* wake up call too. Just as one must step up to the plate and claim their part of the responsibility for seeking solutions, so must all. There is no hiding place and no excuses.

This is a call to the militant groups on both sides of the racial issues, the political issues, the religious issues, and all those other barriers we have erected between the various segments of the Human race. We are the ones who built the walls; it is up to all of us to expend the power necessary to tear them down and replace them with bridges of trust strong enough to support the truth.

It is a cry to those in the educational system to revitalize our schools with positive energy and courses that teach our children real life skills. It is time to let go of what is no longer applicable in today's reality, time to revise an archaic system filled with dusty ideas and false promises. It is time to replace old courses of the past with innovative, skill-based programs that teach people how to develop, according to their individual talents, a life plan that will bring them self-fulfillment and help them become positive contributors to society.

It is time for the politicians to put aside their egos and greed, getting serious about becoming leaders by earning the right to lead from the people they represent. We need to be looking at our entire system of government and revise it to truly reflect the needs and expectations of the society that elects those in positions of power. We need to revise that system and the processes within it that have evolved to the point of political paralysis. It is time for our leadership to develop into models and mentors, supporting the people, rather than people who seek to control, for whatever reasons, the populace for whom and to whom they are responsible.

It is time for religious leaders to stop running clubs based upon exclusivity, ego and money. Theirs is an awesome responsibility, and it is one that has been violated. They deal with people's minds and spirits. They must also become models and mentors of the philosophies they teach. They must assume the responsibility for their actions. They must also earn the trust and respect of the people they lead. There should be a differentiation between profits and prophecy.

Keep church and state separate. They are a dangerous combination in the wrong hands, as history has illustrated so many times. But let's combine moral and societal leadership. Let us seek an innovation in principal-based leadership in all areas, including the corporate world.

Money is power in our societies and nowhere is there so much of it as in the corporate world. It is time for corporations to give back some of the incredible money and power they have earned or stolen from the people back to the very society and culture that has supported them. It is time for corporate management to become leaders and supporters within and outside the walls of their places of business, assuming a responsibility for helping to finance the rebuilding of our society. It is time to re-engineer more than just their processes to improve their individual bottom line profits, and contribute their knowledge, skills and resources toward constructing an environment that is safe, healthy and conducive to the consistent and continuous improvement of quality for all.

All of us, in every society, in every part of the world, have a role to play. We have seen the developments in this world and we have either chosen to be a part of them or chosen to ignore them. Now is not the time for selective ignorance. It is time to broaden our perceptions and grasp the opportunity to make a difference; a difference in your own life and in everyone's life, so that the next significant development will be the development of our personal circumstances, the development of our minds.

TRANSFORMATIONAL THINKING: ITS ROLE IN TRANSFORMING THE WORLD

There is plenty of blame and shame to go around, but that is not the purpose of this book. As long as we continue to point the finger of blame at each other, we will never reach the point of joining hands and coming together to accomplish the task before us. There has been too much of that already. This is a time for solutions, not wallowing in the problems we have all created. It is time for all of us to stop being Victims of Circumstance and become Champions of Change. That is what this approach is all about.

I want to offer some starting points, plant some seeds in the fine minds of people in all segments of our societies, so that we can, individually and collectively, arrive at creative and innovative solutions, bringing all those segments together in a singular purpose: that of creating a commonly shared reality which is inclusive, by nature and design, rather than exclusive and destructive. This is the philosophy of "Transformational Thinking." I believe it contains all the elements necessary to begin the journey toward a holistic healing process that will relieve the suffering and inequity of the reality we have created. I believe it contains the guidelines and skills necessary for all of us to come together on the journey.

It is just as important to define what something is not as it is to explain what it is. Transformational Thinking is not the "end-all and be-all." ("be-all and end-all"???) It is designed to be flexible enough to include the needs and expectations of everybody, containing at least some of the answers we have all been seeking. It is not intended to *supplant* current philosophies, but to *supplement* them. The answers it cannot yet supply can be found as more and more people begin to apply its principles and skills within their own realities, leading us to at least ask the right questions. The understanding of this is exactly the purpose of Transformational Thinking having its own web site (www.transformationalthinking.com) so that the concepts within it can be developed by some of the unheralded minds that are out there, ready to grab the nettles and grapple with the concepts within it.

I do not possess all the knowledge because I am limited by my own perceptions, as we all are. Transformational Thinking is designed to expand the parameters of our own perception as we learn the value of including others' perceptions in the planning, problem solving, and decision-making processes. Through application of the skills within this book, a dialogue between those that read it and the constant understanding and belief that everything can be improved if we approach it from the right angle, Transformational Thinking will develop too, just as it is meant to do. This is why it is simply a seed, designed to give people the skills they need to change their reality, develop themselves and take the whole program to the next level, whatever or wherever that might be.

The world needn't be the way it is. Most importantly *each of our personal worlds needn't be the way they are.* The reality of the planet that we live on and the reality of the life that you find yourself living today is interconnected and inseparable. Everyone has a responsibility and everyone can make a difference. Once we recognize that the root of every problem comes from a thought that someone, somewhere, switched on in their head, then we are armed with the knowledge and primed to tackle the problem. Next, all we need is the resolve.

As the saying goes, everything is created twice, first with the mind, then with the hand. On that basis we must resolve to adapt the mind.

If we are to make a difference, we must transform our thinking. Transform our focus and our approach. We must have goals that reflect our true selves and never give up on trying to achieve them.

TRANSFORMATIONAL THINKING: CHALLENGE ALL ASSUMPTIONS

We must begin the transformational process by challenging ALL of our assumptions. There are no sacred cows here. Everything and everyone is subject to challenge. This is not done with the purpose of destroying them, but to bring them out into the light to look at them. We need to see if they are effective tools, skills and means in today's reality, that will serve the purpose to which we must all dedicate our personal and collective power: that of recreating a commonly shared reality that provides a better quality of life for all members of the human race and paves the way for further and consistent development. It is based upon a recognition and celebration of the human spirit, something we all have in common.

We must begin this process of transformation deep within each and every individual, ever expanding outwards to include others. That process of inclusion reaches out and affects those with whom we have established relationships, whatever those relationships are – personal or professional, based upon mutual trust and respect.

Gradually, as the parameters of our own perceptions are expanded and transformed; as we begin to realize the power of our own decisions and the accompanying responsibility that our choices carry in terms of the effects they create, we will learn the value of including the perceptions of others. This is the true basis of a symbiotic relationship, in which all benefit. This is how to establish and realize the benefits of true synergy.

By simply expanding the parameters of our perception and assuming the responsibility for our own choices and the resultant consequences of our behavior, we begin to live our individual lives with purpose and accountability. A natural increase in sensitivity comes with higher degrees of awareness and consciousness. We start to place a higher significance on our own lives and our relationships. We start to understand that *we do reap what we sow*.

Improving the Quality of the Journey

Transformational Thinking not only provides the seeds for initial sowing, but the skills and tools necessary to sustain that process, consistently and continuously improving the quality of our own lives and those within our sphere of influence. These skills and the principles upon which they are based are universal in application. They can be applied by anyone in any circumstances, regardless of one's starting point on the journey. There are no barriers, only stepping-stones to help us get from where we are to where we could and should be. Moreover, we discover that the true goal is not some nebulous hope and promise in the distant future, but the quality of each step of the journey, here and now.

Keeping it Simple

All too often, approaches to change rely upon the reader having a degree in engineering or psychology to be applied effectively. Transformational Thinking takes a different tack. It is a systematic approach that is simple in concept, easy to learn and also simple to apply, share with and *teach to others*. But do not confuse simplicity with effectiveness. Unnecessary complexity is one of the aspects of the overall problem we need to solve. *Keeping it simple* is one of the keys to its effectiveness.

Simplicity is also one of the keys to the *universal applicability* of the principles and skills contained within this philosophy. I have taught these principles and skills to over forty nationalities throughout the world to people of many cultures, and all walks of life. In virtually every case in which they have been applied, the result is an almost immediate and positive one. When applied consistently, the result is consistent and constant improvement in all aspects of the individual's life or the overall corporate culture. I might also add that, as far as application in the corporate world goes, companies that have applied these principles and skills have experienced an increase in their bottom line profits, as well. I have taught them to children, families and to entire organizations, including everyone in the organization, from the president and CEO to the janitors. When everyone is included and involved in the planning, decision-making and solution-seeking processes, they become committed to the common purpose, united and aligned. They become "a part of" as opposed to "apart from."

Transform

Much of our sense of reality is built around the belief that there will always be enough time to get done what we want to get done. But the hundreds of species that die out on this planet each year would beg to differ. As the harvesting of our trees increases, our forests would beg to differ. As our factories produce more and consume more, the natural resources of this planet would beg to differ. As the divorce rate increases throughout the world, many children would beg to differ.

There is not enough time. There never is. But maybe now we should concentrate our resources on what we can do, not what we can't. Maybe now we must begin to ask ourselves what we can do to change that. Maybe now is the time to ask:

Is it time we all begin to assume the responsibility for improving our own lives and the world in which we live? Is it time to recognize our differences as a source of increased perception rather than barriers? Is it time we all get off our individual and collective butts and begin contributing and constructing rather than denouncing and destroying? Is it time to come together in a sprit of true communication, cooperation, and coordination? Is it time to build upon our strengths and develop our weaknesses? Is it time we recognize and celebrate the human spirit and tap into this incredible source of unlimited potential, redirecting our energy, time, and efforts towards more constructive and meaningful purposes?

Isn't it time for a little Transformational Thinking?

TRANSFORMATIONAL THINKING: HOW IT WORKS

In the next few chapters we will explore the basic concepts of the Transformational Thinking philosophy. We will examine both a system to apply the philosophy we are about to learn in the program, and a few cornerstone concepts that you should understand before setting out to explore the program. These concepts include the process of change, decision making processes, human perception and the concept of Human Spirit.

The Eleven P's

Transformational Thinking is not a difficult concept. For the benefit of simplicity we have broken its main tenets down into a concept of Eleven P's.

Here is how you could look at the concept of Transformational Thinking from the basis of these Eleven P's:

Increased parameters of <u>Perception</u> lead to recognition of full individual and collective <u>Potential</u>. When potential is combined with <u>Principles</u> and <u>Passion</u>, we have created the definition of our beliefs and can commit to maintaining them. When we understand the <u>Politics</u> of relationships and other <u>People</u> are included and involved in matters affecting them, we have common goals that will define our <u>Purpose</u>, to which everyone can commit. We can now formulate <u>Plans</u>, which lead to the creation of <u>Processes</u> that serve to help us attain our goals. The final ingredients are <u>Perseverance</u> and <u>Pliability</u>. These final ingredients provide for the flexibility and strength necessary to ensure sustainable growth and improvement.

OK, so I said I was going to keep it simple. Let's try it another way, with a little less of the bull:

By broadening our horizons (Perception) we can begin to see what our potential really is. If we combine this potential by honestly committing ourselves to taking action, which is consistently fair and ethical (Principles), we can commit ourselves fully (Passion) to a set of beliefs. As we learn about how we communicate and interact with others (Poli-

tics) and can include other people in our thinking, we can define our life goals (Purpose) and plan how to achieve our goals and create methods (Processes) through which we can ensure success. Finally, by not giving up (Perseverance) and being open to change (Pliability) we will be able to sustain our efforts and ensure that we are always headed in the right direction.

That, in two, albeit alliterated paragraphs, is the entire philosophy in a nutshell. I told you it was simple and just couldn't pass up the chance to show you how easy it really is to be dazzled by all the razzmatazz! It may be Eleven P's for the benefit of recall but in reality even this can be simplified!

The point is that Transformational Thinking is simple and I will keep it that way throughout the book. If there are any terms you might not understand, I will explain them, not because I'm patronizing anyone but because, at the end of the day, it isn't about terms and phrases, it is just about whether everyone can understand it and apply it without the use of a Roget's Thesaurus, a dictionary of Engineering terms and a damn good bottle of Scotch! This is supposed to be fun, as well as useful, so if you're not already enjoying it, go stand in the corner until you're so bored that you will.

Go on now…

A Philosophy of Life

Right then, this is for the rest of you who are having bags of fun: This formula can be applied individually and collectively. It is basic and simple enough that you can share it with children, yet powerful enough to challenge even the deepest of thinkers and skeptics. Skepticism is, in fact, a welcomed ingredient, answering the need to constantly *challenge all assumptions*, lest we become too complacent in any of our beliefs. Skepticism is simply one valuable aspect of pliability, one of the Eleven P's of the program.

If one places this formula in the context of the human spirit, we have a powerful philosophy that crosses all barriers and is capable of accomplishing literally anything we set our minds to. We will be discussing the human spirit in greater detail, for it is the human spirit that provides the foundation on which this philosophy is designed to work. Understanding the human spirit amounts to nothing more than understanding the attributes common to each of us as human beings and using that knowledge to appreciate how these attributes work while learning how to make them work for us and not against us. Simply stated, for the time being, when the attributes of the human spirit are violated, the result is negative; when they are recognized and celebrated, the result is positive.

As you can readily see, this is a true philosophy, in that it is a way of life. It is a way of conducting one's own life in such a manner so as to attain personal goals, but can be just as easily applied to relationships and organizations. Likewise, it can be applied to existing systems in order to improve them. You will also appreciate their value on both the personal and the professional levels, for the personal is what drives the professional. This is also a concept that we will discuss further at a later stage.

Now let's look at each of the Eleven P's in a little more detail, just to see what you're getting yourself into...

Paradigm Expansion (Perception)

There is a lot of talk these days about "paradigm shift." I prefer to look upon Transformational Thinking as a tool for "paradigm expansion," building upon the wealth of knowledge already attained through experience. Why reinvent the wheel? Let's simply learn what we can from what we already know and begin the process of expanding that knowledge by opening our minds to innovative and creative ways to improve what we are already doing. This is why Transformational Thinking builds upon a number of thinking concepts that are already in existence and combines them into a powerful force through a consistent and flexible philosophy.

One crucial factor of the Transformational Thinking philosophy is that it is not just a lot of theory. It contains the *skills* and *tools* necessary to translate what we learn into action and therefore reality. In so many arenas of training and learning that I have had the misfortune to experience, the resulting effect of what has been learned is no more than a brief motivational burst of energy that, in the real world, is practically useless. The skills in this book have been field tested in as many diverse areas as you can imagine. I believe, based upon what we have already seen, that we have only begun to scratch the surface of the full transformational potential involved.

It is the inclusion of these skills that brings the knowledge gained out of the realm of worthless, useless, impractical information and into the real world. Action is the transformer. Unless we can readily *apply* knowledge, it will forever remain in the ether of the "nice-to-know," at best. Unfortunately, what is "nice-to-know" is usually about as important as knowing the length of Aristotle's hair. It's a great fact but having learned it, what do I do with it?

You will also note that, rather than most traditional approaches, this is an inside-out process. Transformational Thinking deals with the personal individual first and foremost, believing that it is from the individual that all changes stem. The is why we deal with all three of our human operating systems: *the Belief System*, which is our beliefs as defined by values and perceptions, *the Thinking System* which is the forms of skills that we apply when thinking, and then *the Behavior System*, which is how we actually behave when the first two come together. This is holistic, meaning whole or complete. There is a specific reason and purpose for designing it so.

Change imposed or dictated from the outside or from a person in a position of authority carries with it a price tag of resentment. You may direct me to sit, and I will obey because you are my manager, supervisor, teacher, clergyman, parent, etc.; although I am sitting on the outside, I am still standing on the inside. This is referred to as "malicious obedience." Although you may get me to temporarily behave the way you want me to act, the end result will be negative, taking the shape of psychological divorce in the initial phases, and leading to more active rebellion in its later phases. What is important to note here is that the effect is temporary and subject to change as soon as the person that told you to do it looks away.

A more effective and lasting way to get me to adapt my behavior is to provide me with a reason for doing so. You must convince me that doing so will benefit me. This means approaching and affecting my belief systems. It must also be done in a manner that does not violate my human spirit. Only then will true transformation be achievable. Anything less is a disservice to both of us.

Lateral Thinking vs. Linear Logic (More Perceptions)

There is a commonly accepted assumption that people resist change. Stated as such, this is simply not true. People will not resist change they see as *beneficial* to themselves. In fact, most people welcome change they perceive as adding quality and value to their lives. This is as true for young children as it is for adults. The reason is simple. It is logical. It is sane. We are all seeking to add quality to our lives, whether we are aware of it or not. This is just one of many assumptions we must challenge. Transformational Thinking provides us with the skills we need to accomplish that in a constructive manner.

In examining our belief systems, we need to be asking ourselves what we believe, why, and is it applicable in attaining the goals I have set for myself? This is not performed in a vacuum. We need the necessary thinking tools to accomplish this in a creative manner and accomplish them in the real world. These skills are provided in the form of Lateral Thinking, first introduced by Dr. Edward de Bono in the Sixties, yet still as fresh and applicable as they were then. It never ceases to amaze me what people begin doing with a few simple Lateral Thinking skills. We will be introducing them a little later on. First, it is important to understand why Lateral Thinking is so powerful.

Traditional Western thinking system is based upon linear logic. Whereas linear logic is useful in certain areas of the thinking process, it is almost entirely left brain based, allowing little room for the functioning of the right brain, the seat of creativity. If you look at our educational process, you will readily agree that it teaches, reinforces and rewards linear thinking, often downgrading, suppressing and even punishing creative or innovative thinking.

Consider the natural tendency of the child to dream, to wonder, to allow his or her mind to wander and play with thoughts. We train that natural tendency and potential right out of them. We stress the importance of conformity at the expense of individuality and innovation. We place them in categories and learning tracks (which I prefer to consider "ruts"), and trap them inside the limitations we have placed upon them. The emphasis we place on discipline, conformity and competition in the classroom, may serve to turn out great robots for the purposes of yesterday's assembly line approach still commonly practiced in the corporate world (more on that later, I promise), but does little to teach them life skills, nor does this approach turn out very many creative thinkers.

The addition of Lateral Thinking to our toolbox of cognitive tools is an important and crucial one. If we are indeed in the midst of the "Information Age," and I do not dispute that one iota, and we continue to apply the same thinking skills that got us into this mess in the first place, what good does all this additional input of information do us? As Einstein said, "The definition of insanity is doing the same thing in the same way and expecting different results." We need to adopt additional, supplemental thinking skills that will better serve us, individually and collectively, in re-engineering the culture and society in which we live. I'm sure we could all name a few systems, approaches and processes that we considered somewhat less than sane. Therefore I take Einstein's view that we must change our approach and get "sane".

The recovering addict successfully makes the first step towards recovery when he or she realizes and accepts the fact that, "My best thinking is what got me here." Only then can they begin to open their minds and ears and begin the journey of recovery. We are not unlike the recovering alcoholic or addict. We are reeling from the many illusions with which we have surrounded ourselves. We need to identify and eliminate such illusions before we can successfully deal with the facts.

Look Inwards, Think Outwards (Even more Perceptions)

Part of the process of expanding the parameters of our perception is turned inwards, while the other is extended outwards. For, at some point, we must deal with the decision making process, itself. We must learn to fully appreciate the full power of our decisions, their direct and indirect outward effects, and the fact that we will also have to live with the consequences. This increased awareness, which Lateral Thinking greatly serves to enhance, leads us to make better decisions, based upon a wider preliminary consideration of the consequences than most of us currently practice. I will demonstrate, in several ways, how we usually make decisions, and provide the reader with the skills and knowledge necessary to produce better decisions, plans and solutions in a later chapter.

The externally extended elements of these skills are designed to, not only expand our own perceptions, but to demonstrate the value in including other people's perceptions with our own, thus widening the number of options available to us. This is all based upon a simple natural law called the Law of Requisite Variety, which states that, "the more options from which one has to choose, the more likely one is to make a better decision or choice." As I previously mentioned, the synergy (the concept that the complete article is more powerful than the sum of all its parts) and symbiosis (a natural occurrence of life forms providing mutually beneficial services to one another which sustain the survival of both), which I refer to as "symbiotic synergy," is often astounding. I have never before seen the two concepts of symbiosis and synergy combined, but examination of the results of such a process is exactly what occurs.

That is about the full extent of psychobabble contained in this book. I disdain such "coined" phrases and terminology, but I suppose some of them are inevitable, as they have become imbedded in our thought processes and languages throughout the world. I promise the reader that all such usage will be translated into layman's terms in at least two or three different ways, so that there is no doubt as to their meaning, regardless of whether the reader possesses a degree or not. Even from that perspective, a degree is no more a measure of intelligence than a ruler is a Geiger counter. This is not about intelligence or about how qualified one is; it has to do with thinking ability, something most of us have not received in school, regardless of how far we have gone through an education system that rarely applauds thinking and consistently rewards the reproduction of information in a required format.

As a matter of fact, there is a danger in relying on the intelligence alone for our thinking. De Bono refers to this as the "Intelligence Trap." Lateral Thinking is designed, for the most part, to help us develop our natural, innate, intuitive thinking abilities that we were born with and most of us had educated out of us. Remember the phrases like "Act your age," and "Grow up"?

Personal and Inter-personal Development (Potential)

We will examine potential from many different angles. We will look at our natural internal abilities and talents, both realized and latent; we will be looking at existing, external potential, in the form of what we can gain and learn from our current situation or circumstances, and the people we already know, commonly referred to as networking.

But we will also be looking at how to develop our own potential and that of those around us. This is important from the standpoint of relationships, families, groups, teams and organizations. Development is an essential part of the empowerment process, of which we hear so much and see so little. In so many organizations in which I have worked, I have seen this powerful tool misunderstood, under used and often abused but it is the personal arena where our honesty with ourselves will harness this tool to the greatest effect. We will look at self-empowerment and the empowerment of others. Taken in the context of the human spirit, it is the only sane and effective approach, one that leads to better results through a higher degree of commitment and involvement of all those included.

Special Ingredients (Principles and Passion)

Two other ingredients necessary are principles and passion, though neither of these seems to receive much attention or emphasis in most approaches. I consider them to be crucial parts to the overall process. Principles become the guidelines for our behavior, while passion is the driving force that keeps us on track and full of life.

A lack of clearly defined principles creates unnecessary confusion and conflict, both personally and collectively. Whereas this should really be a no-brainer, (and I will give many of the "experts" the benefit of the doubt on this one), it is precisely the lack of principles, determining what constitutes acceptable and non-acceptable behavior, that creates many problems that could and should never have occurred in the first place. This is particularly true in any human relationship, personal or professional.

Not having clearly defined principles also sets us up for unnecessary failures by establishing expectations for ourselves and others that can never be realized. A quick example of this was the concept of "zero defects" dictated in many Total Quality Management (TQM) programs several years ago which were commonly used in corporations around the world and are, in fact, still in use in some of them today. How many of us are capable of reaching or sustaining perfection? The resultant frustration this concept led to was shocking even to those who introduced it. Now, the currently accepted theory, imported from Japan, is that of Kai Zen, constant and consistent, incremental improvements over the long haul. That is something we can all live with and strive for.

Principles stem from our belief system, but also involve our thinking system. This may be another reason that some of the "experts" have steered clear of this territory. The principles we are speaking of here have nothing to do with religion and everything to do with the human spirit. These are "natural" principles, meaning that they appeal to our instincts as human beings, and serve to establish what constitutes acceptable and non-acceptable behavior for ourselves and within our relationships with others. Once again, clearly establishing these guidelines and the consequences of our behavior eliminates unrealistic expectations and unnecessary conflict.

It is important to understand in the establishment of principles that they be ones with which we can live and commit to practicing. This is where we divide those who just talk the talk from those who walk the walk. "By your actions will they know you," is sage advice here. Professing to believe one thing while practicing another is unacceptable. It is hypocrisy, something which no one trusts and respects. Another common expression that applies here is "To thine own self be true."

Many people confuse values with principles. While we will be getting into the differences between the two, very basically, a value is a broad umbrella, such as "honesty," while under that value, we may have several principles. A value is not specific enough, and as in all areas, the clearer the definition, the better the understanding. You will see that, what a lot of people like to think of as lack of awareness, is really a case of what I refer to as "selective ignorance." Remember that awareness carries with it responsibility. It is easier and more convenient to remain unaware and consequently continue acting in an unprincipled manner, than to choose the path of spiritual responsibility and accountability, which requires individual effort and uncompromising personal commitment. Better to remain a Victim of Circumstance than to assume the Challenge of Change.

Passion is the depth of feeling and emotion we pour into living our life. If you had the power to create any job for yourself, would you not choose to do something you really enjoyed doing, something you were *passionate* about? Unless we are living life with passion we are merely surviving. Passion provides us with the courage of our convictions, eliminating fear and doubt in pursuing a path toward our goals. That is not to say that we should live only to satiate our passions. In this respect, we are more concerned with the ability to get excited about those things to which we are committed. Passion is the force that drives us to perform beyond our own expectations, reaching ever higher and higher plateaus of accomplishment, ever improving, ever evolving.

Politics (No, not Democrats and Republicans)

At this stage in the program, we will have covered Perceptions, Potential, Principles and Passion. Can you see where the elimination of one or another of these ingredients would water down the mixture to create a tasteless, bland existence? Life is meant to be enjoyed, experienced. There is no law that states otherwise. Yet, how many of us are merely surviving? Just hanging on? That is not what the journey is all about. Boring journeys lead to boring goals and minor accomplishments, at best. Who needs that in their life, when we are capable of so much more?

Maybe if we had a few more teachers out there, teaching subjects about which they could feel passionate, and an educational system that rewarded innovation and creativity, rather than conformity and a grading system that recognizes one's ability to parrot what one is being taught, we would have more students staying in a process that is challenging and exciting, rather than escaping from the boredom and stifling atmosphere that currently exists. I remember speaking to, or more importantly, *listening* to my eight-year old nephew when he was saying, "Why don't they teach us stuff in school that we can use?" I didn't offer much more than a feeble reply, not wishing to display my frustrations and further entrench his disappointment and frustration. If an eight-year old boy can see things so clearly, why can't we listen? Do you know what we had been discussing that led up to his statement? Lateral Thinking.

Well, the opening few salvos in this book are all leading up to the definition of our purpose in life. However, before we are able to begin defining our purpose in life, we must deal with two elements of Transformational thinking that will surely have a dramatic effect on how successful we will be achieving our purpose(s). These are Politics and People.

Politics, in this instance, has nothing to do with the political establishments that we all know and love. I am not suggesting you run for congress or parliament or whatever the name of your particular political establishment may be (but don't let me stop you!), this is all about human interaction and the political relationships we have among those people we know.

Getting things done through other people is a straight-talking way of demonstrating what politics really is. We all do it, every day when we ask a friend to pass the salt shaker, give us a lift home, or pick up an extra pack of cigarettes to save us going ourselves. But this form of interaction between people is too often taken for granted simply because it is something that seems to come naturally to us. After all, humans communicate all the time, we learn our languages, go about talking, writing and communicating with one another and everything works our wonderfully, right? Yes, well, sometimes anyway…

The Fifth 'P', Politics, looks at a few skills that we will need when we really start putting our Purpose(s) into action a little later on. *Listening*, for example, is a hugely under-rated skill, with the vast majority loving to talk but very few of us willing or capable of listening as well as we might. This all causes confusion, frustration and a lot of grief that is all avoidable. How often do we listen and wish the person would get to the end of the sentence while they blah, blah, blah, blah, blah, blah…

There is so much room for error and misunderstanding that Goethe, the German philosopher, was once quoted as saying, *"No one would talk much if they knew how often they misunderstood others"*. Therefore, if we are to understand others and develop the full potential of the relationships that exist around us just waiting to be developed, we must learn to understand others more, by listening and having a proactive approach to communication.

This is just a foundation for what follows, because the art of good relationships isn't just about communication, it is based upon seven principles that we will need to look into in order that we can apply them to ourselves, before we begin applying them to others.

As we work through the Transformational Thinking system, you will quickly see the nature of improvement that I am proposing. In order that we make effective changes to improve our realities, we must not only be honest with ourselves and strive to improve the way we perceive the world, but also begin treating others as we would like to be treated ourselves. Since none of us are islands, as so eloquently pointed out by Thomas Merton, we must all live in streets, in communities, in cities and countries across the world that make a planet into a home for our race and the millions of species upon it. Sometimes, we are prone to forget that and we act in selfish and harmful ways that are destructive to others and, most importantly in the context of this program, to ourselves.

If we are seeking to develop ourselves, we must look into these relationships and choose to adapt our behaviors so that they are not harmful to others but fruitful and generous of spirit, which, as will be illustrated in 'The Pebble in the Pond' later on, will reflect in how others treat us. These foundations will be vital to advancement in the program and in the improvement of the reality that we are looking for.

Everyone We Meet, We Learn From (People)

Once we have determined our own perceptions, potential, principles and passions and learned some of the basic rules for communicating effectively within positive relationships, we can then begin to align with other people. Does that mean that we should only seek those with the same perceptions? Absolutely not! Different perceptions help us to continue expanding our awareness and potential.

It is not just people we agree with that can help us. We cannot wrap ourselves in cotton wool and go out and meet only those people that agree with us. That is not a lesson of life, nor is it an element of Transformational Thinking.

People really enter into the picture at every phase of this Transformational Thinking, as they do in life in general, but I have chosen to include a chapter on it at this point in the program for the purpose of introducing a form of networking that I hope you will find greatly increases your potential. But it is not just what we can get from other people that is important. Quality of life can be reflected in the quality of those around us too, just as in the section on Politics, we will look at the quality of the relationships we hold and determine what transfers of assistance and companionship can be developed within them.

I always look at another human being and wonder what he or she is here to teach me. I will talk to anyone who has the time. I enjoy listening to other people's perceptions, concepts and ideas, regardless of how different from my own they might be. By approaching people with this attitude of respect for their human spirit, I learn consistently and continuously, and it is wonderful. The concept of approaching people with this attitude is one we will explore further as we go deeper into the concept of Transformational Thinking.

There are, admittedly, some people who are a negative influence. These are people that I simply shut out of my life after all attempts to turn the situation around have been ineffective. Notice that I didn't say "failed?" That is because I do not believe that any experience or person we learn from is a failure. I hear people talk about "failed relationships," "failing" at this or that, and I always ask them what they have learned or can find in the situation that will help them improve their life. There is always a lesson in there if we look with eyes that see or listen with ears that hear or think with minds that seek to understand.

From a business point-of-view, people are what virtually every business should be about. The people to whom we are selling this product or providing that service, the people who sell or deliver it, and the people who buy or want the service we are offering. I spent several years working of a marketing firm that worked on processes instead of people. How many times do we concentrate on the processes and not the people performing them? You want to improve your processes? Develop your people to the point that you can involve and include them in doing so. It is all about people, people!

We talk about the "educational system," the "political system," the "justice system," and what are we really talking about? People. We can't figure out why we can't fix all these systems. It is because we are concentrating on the wrong purpose. The purpose of all the above is *people*.

We wonder why we have so many problems in the corporate world. It is because we are still trying to practice techniques that are no longer effective in today's reality. Processes are meant to be managed; people are meant to be led and supported. Yet all too often, just the opposite is the reality; people are secondary to the processes. If our corporations would spend a fraction of what they are spending on "process improvement" programs on "people development" programs, the processes would end up being improved by the very people who know the processes better than most management personnel, simply because they are the ones performing them day after day. You want to get some commitment out of your people? Get them involved. People are the greatest asset of any business. That is as true of the employee as it is of the customer. Want your customers taken care of? Take good care of your people. It is that simple.

(In case you hadn't noticed, I am a bit passionate on this subject, as well. Did I mention the fact that I love people? Thought I might have dropped a hint a few paragraphs or so ago.)

In fairness, people have become more of a corporate focus in recent times but I sense it is something of a charade. They've tried every other approach, what's left? Oh yeah, those people that make it, deliver it and buy it! Perhaps we should focus on them! Sarcasm aside, this is another reference to the personal driving the professional. Corporations are all too ready to push the professional envelope, substituting professional development for personal when the reality is that the actual person is secondary to the interests of the corporation. Sadly, the reality is that the personal development of the individual would deliver far greater rewards. Alignment of purpose? How about a corporation's alignment with an employee's purpose? How often had your company wondered what your dreams were? You know the corporate Mission Statement? Does the corporation know yours? I doubt it, which is why there is still so far to go for corporations putting people first and not selfish interests.

Mixing the Mix (Purpose)

What have the first 6 P's established? By this point in the program you will have done the groundwork for all that follows. As we will discover in Perceptions, the very first chapter of the program, much of what we believe to be true is all a matter of how much information we have to confirm our own opinions. It may not actually bear much resemblance to the truth at all. From *Perceptions* to Potential to *Principles* to *Passion*, to *Politics* and to *People*, you will have learned skills that will help to broaden your perceptions, give a sense of pattern in your life and prepare you to begin defining your *Purpose*.

The ability to perceive and establish one's purpose(s) in life is fundamental to leading a life that is filled with meaning and significance. Purpose answers the basic question that we begin asking almost as soon as we can speak. *"WHY?"* (Spend some time with a two-year old to receive confirmation of that observation.) It is a question to which many go to their graves never having discovered an adequate reply. But what kind of traditional answers do our adult mentors give the child, and later the student, still later the employee? *"Because I said so. That's why."*

Sorry! Thanks for playing our game, but that is an incorrect answer...

(Contestant exits stage left)

Often even those claiming to have the answers are simply repackaging that reply in different guises. This is exhortation without explanation, which leads to frustration. There ought to be a reason for everything we do. As we shall see, one of the attributes of the human spirit is that we are *purpose beings*. We *need* to know why. This is necessary, not "nice to know" information. Without clearly defined purpose(s), how can we plan the journey? It is our guiding star by which we navigate. We have to know what we hope to accomplish before we can begin placing one foot in front of the other.

A favorite exercise of mine that I use when working with organizations is to have everyone close their eyes and point to true north, asking them to keep their arms extended. Then I have them open their eyes. It is an exercise that never fails to bring laughter and always permits me to drive the point home. Arms are pointing in every direction. That is how many people within a company perceive their vision and mission. There is no clearly defined purpose.

Another that I use when working with senior management individuals is to have them write down and prioritize what they consider to be the five purposes of the organization or company. It is amazing how few of those lists match those of the others, all tasked with leading their various departments or teams in the same direction. Is it any wonder that the people they are leading are often operating at crossed-purposes?

The same is true in relationships. How many relationships fail because of a simple lack of alignment in purpose? She wants one thing, he wants another, the children come in between and very quickly the relationship breaks down simply because the alignment of purpose has self-destructed! This, of course isn't limited to our life partners but extends to our friends, our families, our casual acquaintances and indeed, everyone that we come into contact with throughout our lives.

In order to begin addressing these situations, we need to define our *individual* purpose first, then the pieces of the puzzle will gradually fall into place. We can begin to relate to other people with similar purposes, work with a company that mutually benefits both parties, look at global issues with a broadened perspective of what the answers to those issues should encompass, right on down the line, from internal to external in a ever-widening net.

I recently turned down a very generous business offer for the simple reason that the commitment involved did not fit in with my life plan, which is based upon the purposes I have defined. How did I arrive at those purposes? They are simply a combination of my perception, potential, principles, passion, politics and people. I know what I am supposed to be doing, because I know where I am going. I have established my personal vision and mission in this life. I see it clearly. I believe in it and in my own potential to attain it. I am passionate about it. And principles will not permit me to commit to something I know I may not be able to deliver. Sometimes this seems to be challenged, perhaps by the size of the salary we are offered, or the location of the job or the sense of the "once in a lifetime opportunity". But once these concepts are clearly defined in your mind you'll know that however juicy the cherry may look, if it's not in alignment with your purpose, if it does not fit in with your perception, potential, principles and passion, it is simply a poisoned chalice. It may be bearable for the reason that you took the opportunity but, as we have already covered, who wants life to be merely 'bearable'? It's a ride. A roller coasting, barnstorming ride that we're supposed to revel in. If we compromise that, what are we really doing? Just riding the current in a shallow river devoid of the big fish we set out to hook.

I see so many people of all ages and educational levels, hopelessly wandering through life with no passion or purpose. Though some of these people may have found their way to financial success, internally, they are not content. They are bored or frustrated. They have no idea what to do next to bring joy and a sense of self-fulfillment into their lives. They lack a purpose and passion. They are souls lost at sea in a dense fog. They confuse what they want with what they need. How can one determine one's needs until one knows where one is headed? If I know where my journey is going to take me, I will know what to pack.

I see other people, many financially well off and just as many financially challenged, who are going through their lives with a sense of happiness and self-fulfillment. These are people who know what their journey is all about and have either progressed pretty far along the path, or are content that they are at least on schedule, right where they are supposed to be. Though some may look at the latter group and say that they are simply blissful in their ignorance, I would argue that, in most cases, just the opposite is true. These are people who understand their true purpose in life. The ignorance, in this case, is in the eyes of the beholder.

But, as you will have learned by this point in the program, none of the Eleven P's act independently of one another, they are all interconnected and flexible. We will link purpose to those people with which we surround ourselves, recognizing how an alignment of purpose between people, groups or organizations is highly powerful and effective.

Purpose is fundamental to our growth and equally detrimental should we not properly define it. At every stage in defining our purpose, we include others in the factors that we consider. When we can combine our purpose with another person's our strength is doubled and the politics and people skills that we will learn will dovetail in a powerful toolkit of skills.

Who Brought the Map? (Plans)

Plans. A person without a plan is a boat with no sails, oars, or motor, drifting helplessly with the currents and tides. The captain may spot landfall, but only luck is going to get him there. Once one has established purpose, now we can set about making plans. Plans are the stepping-stones that get us to the overarching purpose. Here again, Lateral Thinking can offer much and serves this purpose particularly well.

You know what they say about the best-laid plans of mice and men. Plans change because situations and circumstances change. We may go to step on this stepping-stone and find it is a bit shaky. Better to withdraw one's foot before applying full weight on it and start looking around for an alternative. Otherwise, we could end up getting soaked in the water. Here, pliability rears its head too, serving notice of the interconnected nature of the Eleven P's. But more about pliability later...

Why do I place people and politics before plans? As I said earlier, people really belong throughout, but people who are involved and included in the planning process are more likely, first of all, to provide additional insight; and secondly, to commit to the plan. Again, I want to re-emphasize that we do not live or operate in a vacuum. Our decisions affect other people. Here, I refer to relationships on both the personal and professional levels.

Good, sound planning is a skill. It can be taught and learned. I feel we should be teaching it to our children at a much earlier age. How much training and development effort is directed towards teaching this crucial skill in the early years, before ineffective habits are formed? Not enough, I am afraid. Planning is a life skill. I meet people of all ages and backgrounds who haven't a clue on how or where to start a plan. Is it any wonder such people get lost on the journey? It is not a difficult skill to teach. It is so vital and important in attaining the purpose(s) we set, yet I have actually had people tell me that they do not have enough time to plan! I always ask if they are going to have enough time later on to clean up the mess their lack of planning is bound to create. Needless to say that they all think they'll get it right first time without a clue where they're headed, what they're going to do when they get there or how the hell to extricate themselves from the mess when the whole thing goes belly-up!

The Planning Chapter will give you the opportunity to begin designing your Dream Job. Through examining your life's purpose you can bring to bear the skills and tools you will have learned to this point and begin truly creating a plan to bring your purpose to fruition. We will also look at planning how to achieve your other life purposes and give you some tools and guidelines to take them out of the realm of dreams and actualize them in your reality. This chapter asks some questions that will have far-reaching effects on the state of your reality and what you are going to do about improving it. Here, the rubber begins to hit the road, and you are in the driving seat!

Step-By-Step (Processes)

Proper planning creates smoother processes. Flexibility, built into the planning stage, complete with measurements and all that other good stuff, will provide us with the ability to improve the processes as changes in circumstances suggest. I have never met a process yet that couldn't be improved upon. Just when you think you have it down to perfection...zap! Here comes another change. Life is a process of dynamic change, why should our plans be any different, and why shouldn't our processes be as flexible as the environment in which they are designed to work? Who better to spot the need for change and make the suggestions on what to tweak here and adjust there than the people performing the processes? In this case, that person is you. See, it is all interconnected.

Processes are the translation of all that has come before, putting the Perception, Potential, Passion, Politics, People, Purposes(s) and Plans, into action. They are what make it all smoothly come to life. It is in the stage of applying all the knowledge and skills we learned in the previous stages that we actually create the reality in which we live. It is the "doing" part. This is where we get in, roll up our sleeves and get to work, making it all happen. Providing we have applied ample attention and care to all the other phases or steps, the processes should be easier to accomplish.

Specifically, we will be looking at some of the processes in your life that may not be working out. I will give you some tools, particularly those from TQM, which will help you to define root problems in the processes that all our lives are constructed from. We will look at how to define problem statements and how to get to the solutions that will eliminate the reoccurrence of the problem. In practical terms, this is a smoothing-out solution, looking for where the blips are occurring and looking for practical and sustainable solutions to improve the general quality of our reality.

Rowing with Rubber Oars? (Perseverance and Pliability)

Now it comes down to perseverance and pliability, the latter which we have already made several references to. Perseverance is a lot easier when we are all rowing in the same direction, supporting one another. It means maintaining our spirit and energy levels when times are tough, as well as when times are good, though I have rarely seen the latter included in most approaches.

The need for perseverance is more obvious when things are going against you, when you are swimming against the current; but perseverance is also necessary during the boom times, when things are going great. Without it, we become complacent and good is really the enemy of best. We need to be just as alert, looking for ways to grow and improve during these times, for this is when we are most likely to let our guard down, relax, sit back and take it easy.

Pliability is based upon another of De Bono's concepts, that of Water Logic vs. Rock Logic. Water Logic is being flexible enough to be willing to change ourselves, our perception, and all the rest of it, as conditions change. Too often, even though we may say we subscribe to the old adage that "nothing is set in stone," we are more like stone than stone itself, hard, immovable, unyielding, unbending, stubborn. (I am sure I could come up with a few more adjectives, but I am sure you get the idea.)

Pliability is what ensures consistent and continuous improvement. It applies to all the aspects of this philosophy, from perception right on through to processes. It also completes the cycle and spirals it upwards one more notch, for pliability is the means to attaining consistently higher and higher plateaus until we have achieved what I define as success, and that is self-fulfillment.

Although pliability is the final ingredient, it takes us back to the beginning of the spiraling cycle, if there is such a thing as a beginning. I do know that, as long as I live, there will never be an end. After that, who knows? And that brings us back to a point I wish to re-emphasize at the risk of redundancy (said Tom, repetitively): *The quality of the journey is the goal.*

Assume the Truth is an Assumption

That is how the Transformational Thinking system works. Now, to answer questions I would be asking if I were you: *Assuming* Transformational Thinking works, how can I make it work in my life? How can I use it to transform my reality? What's in it for me? How do I get the most benefit from this book?

In case you did not notice, that last paragraph contained an assumption, a mighty large one. We said, "Assuming Transformational Thinking works..." That is the first suggestion: *Challenge all assumptions.*

It is important that we accept nothing at face value. It is equally as important to realize that we each have individual needs and expectations. Though we all share commonalities, i.e., we all belong to the human race etc. each of us must choose our own path of personal power.

I cannot overstress the importance of challenging assumptions. We will be doing a lot of it, so it is equally vital that we approach the task of doing so with the right frame of mind. The purpose of challenging assumptions is not to destroy them, punch holes in them, or anything else of a like nature. The purpose is to learn as much as we can about the assumptions before personally committing to this decision, that course of action, one path of life, another goal or objective, or whatever. It is an approach that is intended to be constructive, as opposed to destructive, supplemental (adding to), as opposed to "supplanting" (replacing with), paradigm transformation as opposed to paradigm shift.

I cannot remember a single experience in any form of learning that I have encountered in my life where the teacher has asked us, implored us, to question what we are learning. Usually truth is considered implicit in the act of learning but this is just one more assumption that we should, *must* challenge. If we are to embark on this journey together, questioning the assumptions that we have made about our view of reality and the choices we have made that have got us here, then how can I credibly ask you to not to challenge the assumption that Transformational Thinking works? I cannot and I will not. The proof of the pudding, as they say, is in the eating.

The Parable of the Raft

Gautama, the Buddha, was teaching one day. There was a heckler in the crowd that used to follow him from place to place, trying to trick him with deeply loaded questions. On this particular day, he asked Gautama, "Are you telling us that your way is the only way?"

Gautama recognized this as a loaded question He knew if he answered " yes," then he would be accused of being a god, a falsehood, which he didn't want to impart to anyone. If he answered "no," the heckler would accuse him of not having a message of real value. So he decided to answer a question with a story:

"A man is on a long journey. In the course of his journey, he comes upon a body of water that is too wide to swim across and too long to go around. He knows his goal lies beyond the far shore, but is at a temporary loss as to how he can reach that distant shore. He decides to sit beneath the shade of a stand of bamboo trees and meditate on his problem.

"Suddenly, he gets an idea. Standing up, he takes out his knife and begins to fashion a raft from a few of the bamboo trees. Using the raft and his own power (an important factor in this man's journey), he eventually attains the far shore.

"Now, the question is: What does the man do with the raft? Should he pick it up and carry it upon his back just in case he might encounter another body of water? Or, now that the raft has served its purpose, should he leave it behind and continue on his journey unburdened?"

The heckler thought about the question posed to him and replied, "Surely he would be a fool to carry this heavy raft around on his shoulders for the rest of his life! He must leave it behind."

Gautama replied, "So it is with my teachings. As long as they assist you in the attainment of your goal, use them. As soon as they become a burden, discard them."

Journey

It is my sincere hope that the reader, regardless of your starting point on the journey or your eventual goals, will find within the philosophy of Transformational Thinking, some of the elements (bamboo trees) necessary to assist you in attaining those goals. It is my sincere belief, based upon my own personal experience and those of the countless others who have been directly or indirectly exposed to these principles and skills, that you will, indeed, find something of value here.

But remember, like the man in the story, we must each apply our own personal power in order to cross our rivers. That is a crucial element to the story. Having the raft, but expecting the raft, and the raft alone, to get one to the other side, doesn't work. Real, conscious effort and application of the knowledge and skills of Transformational Thinking does. No matter how good and sturdy the raft, without the additional dynamic of one's personal power, one is bound to be swept downstream by the prevailing winds and currents.

I have built into this concept the very pliability that I believe we will all need to complete our journeys, wherever that personal destination may be. If we take Gautama's words at face value, we can see that there is no such thing as single truth. The journey of Transformational Thinking is the journey of the man with the raft and your river will be personally yours, your truth, and yours alone. It will certainly take you somewhere, if you apply it well, and it will certainly give you the skills you need to improve the quality of that journey. However, as I have insisted upon throughout, it is only together, developing and building upon it, that we can reach an understanding of how to modify and perfect the system day to day, in an ever changing world, where perfection may exist but if it does, it will be fleeting and temporary. Only together, working with mutual trust and respect, can we be aligned in purpose and working towards the same goals of improving the system to meet the modern challenges that grow anew with each day. By tackling our personal realities we will begin to improve the reality of everyone around us. The irony is that, however different our realities may be, I believe that Transformational Thinking will give us the commonality to talk the same language, agree to listen to one another's differences, and learn how to make a better collective reality from each other.

With that, I invite you: use Transformational Thinking to achieve your goals, improve your reality and develop the quality of your life. But a word of warning: from here on in, you may have to change.

I know. It would be scary if it wasn't so much fun...

The Process of Transformation

I don't know where the expression, "people resist change," came from. Nor do I really care. The time, energy and effort wasted in tracking down the originator of this expression, on which so many false assumptions have found their way into our individual and collective belief systems, would be tantamount to trying to find the mother lode of iron pyrite, more commonly called "fool's gold." It simply doesn't matter. What does matter is that there are a lot of people who still ascribe to this theory, conducting themselves and their dealings with others within their sphere of influence as if it were true.

I would guarantee, however, that whomever this expression could be traced to, had a tradition of trying to impose change on others from a position of authority or externally. Now that is change that most people do resist and, from that perspective, the expression is true. The important point to realize here is that there are different types of change. The expression is not universally applicable to all of them.

There is a great more wisdom about the nature of change expressed in the simple "Serenity Prayer." Many of you will have heard it before:

"God, grant me the serenity to accept the things I cannot change, the courage to change the things that I can, and the wisdom to know the difference."

This simple prayer contains so many morsels and nuggets of gold within it that I feel it is more worthy of our exploration.

First of all, it refers to serenity, courage and wisdom. All three of these are excellent attributes to possess when one is attempting to deal with change. Secondly, it mentions that there are some things over which we have no power whatsoever to change; and there are other things that we have the power to change. Lastly, the implication is certainly here that resisting change over which we have no control does involve a certain lack of wisdom.

Wisdom, as it is defined by the Serenity Prayer, is simply the recognition and intelligence to perceive the different types of change and to thereby guide our actions, emotions and mental attitude toward them differently. Whereas wisdom also implies that there is a need for acceptance of those changes over which we have no control, just the opposite is true when it comes to dealing with issues of change over which we do have control. Again, implied in the simple second section of this prayer, is the thought that we need courage to change the things we can. This implies action. It implies a proactive approach that carries with it a responsibility to step up to the plate and make the changes we see as necessary.

So how does one know the difference? And what establishes that difference between the two types of change: that which we can control and that which we cannot? How does one attain the wisdom necessary to deal with these two different types of change? These are some of the questions that we need to look at, examine and seek to comprehend before we can even consider becoming Champions of Change.

Without getting into a lot of unnecessary analysis, dissecting this thing ad nauseam until we have lost sight of the purpose of the exercise, we do need to begin the discussion with a simple, straightforward understanding of change. Obviously, there are two types: that which we can change, and that which we cannot. In other words, there are those changes over which we have influence and can, through courage and active participation, have an effect or impact on; and there are those that impact on us.

People Power

The starting point is deceptively simple. It involves people. I am responsible for changing the things inside myself; I am not responsible for changing other people outside myself. Understanding and accepting this difference is not as simple as it may seem at first glance. Confusing the two, or lacking the "wisdom to know the difference," would appear to be the key to many of the problems we encounter in life. In order to truly appreciate the full extent of one's personal power to effect real and meaningful change, it is important to understand and to possess the "wisdom to know the difference."

Let us get one thing straight right now. We each possess enough personal power to change anything inside of us that we desire to change. Now, some might consider that to be a sweeping statement, but it is the key to moving out of the realm of being a Victim of Circumstance and into that of becoming a Champion of Change. I will readily admit that there are deep, psychological problems, or chronic conditions that we may need some professional help with but, in the final analysis (pun intended), we are the ones who supply the power to get that raft to the far shore. For some, it may require the assistance of supporting programs and other people and, believe me, I am the first to admit that, but all these external sources of power serve to bolster, reinforce and encourage the development of the internal, individual power of the human spirit. One of the problems that occurs without this realization is the exchange of one crutch for another, still leaving a crippled human spirit in its wake.

If we look back at our paragraph regarding the responsibility for change, let's focus in on the concept of external, negative changes and pressures. What is our reaction to them? What can we do internally about them? For one thing, we can, through increased parameters of awareness, determine and direct our reaction to them and the resultant reply, either in word or deed. This is an internal process that only the person involved has control over. It all boils down, eventually, to individual choice and decision. In other words, you don't make me angry; I choose to react in an angry way, either because my limited perception doesn't see any other options, or because I see them and choose to take the path of anger, regardless. This matter of personal decision and choice (despite sometimes feeling that we have little option but to go a little nuts once in a while!) we will explore in more detail later.

Another problem that arises from the case of limited perception is the setting of unrealizable expectations, either for ourselves or for others. This is a common occurrence in high achievers. The end result is either tremendous elation at having accomplished the impossible, or a horrible depression at having failed. When we have established and imposed expectations for others, we rarely see the poor results achieved as a consequence of our having set expectations that were unattainable for them, in other words, our problem; we have more of a tendency to blame and shame them. Increased perception changes that through an almost imperceptible process that is internal, but with tremendous external manifestation.

What changed? Simply our perception, but the results are incredible.

Attitudes and Perceptions

We can change our attitude. We can change an attitude, which is nothing more than an extended emotion over a longer period of time, through increased perception not only of other people, places and events, but our own reaction to them by the choices we make. A simple attitude adjustment can make the world of difference, not only to how we view ourselves, but how we view those same external forces in the guise of other people, places and events. It is not they who change, merely our perception of them. Even if you put down this book right now and never pick it, or any other book like it, up again, you will change whether you like it or not. The trick is not to accept this passive approach to your development. Many people are unhappy in their lives purely because of this attitude. They've changed so much, so passively, that they simply don't even like themselves anymore! My approach is to get active, to recognize the problems and start sorting them out. The first step is to change our perceptions and start looking at each of these problems differently, with a new, fresh and clear perspective.

For this example I want to refer to an alien visitor, coming to Earth in his spaceship. He lands with the pure intention of knowing what human beings are. Unfortunately for this young and naïve alien, he lands in Germany during World War 2. He sees the gassing of Jews, the destruction of Europe through the blitzkrieg and the misery of violence that raged there for 5 long years. He leaves, thoroughly disgusted with the bellicose and barbaric race he has discovered. He returns to his planet and tells his people of the tribes that killed and maimed with no mercy on that planet called Earth.

His brother was unsettled by this description of a race that he'd seen through TV pictures that his race had taken, of the wonderful blue planet (OK, give me a break!) and couldn't believe that such a terrible race could exist in a place so beautiful. So, he heads off on his own little excursion to Earth to check his brother's perception of the race he'd developed his own opinions about. Landing in Czechoslovakia during the same great war his brother had described he goes in search of the truth. There he visits the factory of one 'Oscar Schindler' and sees a different part of humanity's tragic history. He sees a man who would risk his life for the lives of others that had no shield between them and a war machine engineered to destroy them. He sees a munitions factory designed never to produce a single weapon that could destroy the human beings it was meant to obliterate. He sees a different perspective. He then leaves Earth, his perception of mankind modified by his experience and decides to return again to gather more information.

The question is: which brother was correct? They both had a version of reality that they had perceived and from this perspective had formed an attitude regarding the nature of humanity. Of course, the brother with more information was more correct. And that is the point. He modified his attitude towards humans by simply broadening his perceptions, or more simply put, by gathering more information in order to see the reality for what it truly was.

This is the purpose of broadening our perceptions and adjusting our attitudes. Although my alien tale is a simplification of the process, it serves its purpose by illustrating to us that our attitudes and opinions about things can be changed, and must be changed, if we are to develop a better understanding of the world about us and begin looking at our experiences with an open mind. We can either be passive, and accept our view of the world from what we already know, or in the case of the second alien, take what he had learned from his brother and modify his viewpoint by gathering more information and looking at the issue from a different perspective. Whatever we find from looking at the reality, whether good, bad, or indifferent, we are arming ourselves with a greater and broader perception of reality by keeping an open mind and allowing our attitudes to change with the intake of new information and experiences. The second brother didn't reject what he saw because it conflicted with what he already knew, he didn't get upset about it because the first brother's information had been incomplete, he simply took on board all that he saw and modified his attitude through his experience. We can choose to learn and grow through our experiences, including the painful and hard ones, or we can choose to wallow in them. The difference in results far outweighs the amount of effort involved: a simple change within ourselves.

Responsibility for Changing Others

Can we change other people? Not through a conscious effort and without a heavy price tag. Changing others directly requires the institution of discipline and punishment systems that people, not unreasonably, resent. Just look at the criminal justice systems that imprison people for their crimes. Although this is politically and socially accepted as being the most reasonable method of instituting reform, what does it actually achieve? There are many factors involved in why people re-offend after leaving prison, but it is clear from the high percentage of re-offenders that the fear of incarceration is not one of the major influences encouraging the desired effect of ex-offenders becoming responsible and law-abiding contributors to society. We will not go into great depth regarding the complicated issue of incarceration as a system for behavioral reform but from my own experience implementing Transformational Thinking programs in juvenile detention centers in the United States, I can tell you that, from this perspective, reform comes from the individuals involved having different options, different perceptions and, most importantly, the skills to change themselves.

Another example is in our schools where we can supplement the word "change" for "development" We mold our children into specific human patterns and templates rather than teach them how to personally develop their own interests, talents and future. We focus on "changing" our children into "adults" but give them few options for what they will eventually end up doing anyway, which is developing themselves. The streams of facts and figures that we teach do little in the way of actually developing our children into being healthy-minded, responsible members of our societies. We accept that, as these young people develop into adults, they must, and will, take responsibility for their own development. But schools are focused on producing one type of person, and that is the type to be led and to conform. Why don't we offer our young people the tools and skills they need for success? Thus, this book.

These two examples of institutionalized thinking illustrate that our road towards change must begin internally, in the minds of our people. The systems will come later as people begin to recognize the fact that we cannot change people who do not want to change and, additionally, we do not have the responsibility for doing so. We can lead the horse to water, but we can't make it drink, as the saying goes.

The onus of our change must therefore be on ourselves. This doesn't mean that we can't effect positive and proactive change in others but we must encourage it indirectly through changing ourselves and becoming models and mentors of the behavior we desire. We can change how we treat other people and allow them to treat us. We can change our behavior and attitudes towards them, and this is often enough to "bring them a little closer to the performance or behavior desired." For example, instead of berating them and riding them, we can choose to take a different approach and recognize their achievements, sharing in a celebration of their accomplishments, thereby encouraging more of the same.

Taking Back Control

There will always be people, places and events over which we have no obvious method of control, another element in the "wisdom to know the difference" category. A simple decision to eliminate them from our life or change the way we view them can make a great difference in our own peace of mind and serenity and shifts the emphasis of control from what they do to us from the outside to what is actually happening to us, inside. There will always be people in positions of control over us, whether they be teachers, parents, supervisors, etc. Although we may not always be in a position to change the functional hierarchy created by these situations, such as the relationships involved (teacher/student, parent/child, employer/employee), this does not mean that we must relinquish our own right to happiness and peace by allowing them to control us inside as well as out. Although we may not be able to change the relationship itself, we can change our perception of the other dynamics involved. For example, we may not "like" the teacher, but we can love the person bringing us the knowledge, focusing our attention and intention on the subject, rather than on the person delivering it. By the way, it is even possible to separate the person from their actions, if we are aware enough and possess the thinking tools, the willingness and the courage to do so. This is all part of the process of taking back the control and responsibility for our own reality by perceiving them in a different way and thereby reacting to them in a different way. The results are always positive and that is the overarching purpose of this exercise and the enormous power wielded by our perceptions.

It is even possible to love the person while, at the same time, abhorring their actions. Is it an easy task? If it were, we would have a lot more people practicing a lot more restraint than we do, but the fact that it is possible to do so carries with it a tremendous message for all of us. This is the wisdom of which serenity is created. It douses the fires inside and leads us to much higher plateaus of internal and external accomplishment by allowing us to focus our personal power on what is really important: the way we choose to deal with those actions.

Transformational Thinking: Historical Baggage

Transformational Thinking can be of wonderful benefit in realizing, recognizing and developing your own potential. We are capable of so much more than we give ourselves credit for. Why is that? Because we have allowed ourselves to become Victims of Circumstance. In the Transformational Thinking system, our goal is to recognize the huge power we each posses to alter the

reality of our own world and consequently the world that we all inhabit together. It is not about muttering the mantras of hope, it is about *real, defined, systematic change* that we can all adopt and the power that we possess to deliver in spades. If we can firstly recognize this potential through broadening our perceptions and seeing the true nature of the reality we are living in, what are we actually achieving? It is armchair evolution! An evolving reality simply starting with the recognition of a few factors that have entwined our futures with the mistaken victims we have been in the past. It needn't be that way, as I have proven through my experiences. The first step is simply to broaden the mind and perceive more of the truth, more perception, a better quality of perception, a greater ability to handle the enhanced control that comes with it.

If you are unhappy with your current situation or conditions, then you can change it. Never let anyone else tell you any differently. You have the power to do so. It exists within the innate power of the human spirit, something we all bring into this world with us and something no one can ever take away from you, once you have learned to appreciate and tap into it. Transformational Thinking provides you with the skills to both perceive and to utilize your full personal power. It all begins with a moment of choice.

Let's take a look at the process of change and how it works. Again, you will find that our approach is very simple. Though I am sure there are many more complicated breakdowns of this process, it is in the simplicity of this approach that I have found it applicable within the reality of today. I believe in keeping it simple.

I may have mentioned that…

We Hope You Will <u>Never</u> Be All You Can Be

First, I would like to introduce to what is referred to as the Tension Differential Factor. There are several things to take notice of in this simple model. The first is that it indicates that we are involved in an ever-changing process. This process is what we commonly refer to as *life.* The next is that there is always this *gap* between that *which we want or need to accomplish and where we are.* Note also that the direction indicated is an upward movement. This serves to show us that *we are involved in a growing process.* That is what change should be taking us towards: ever-higher plateaus of learning and development. As we shall see, we can exercise a greater degree of control over that direction, the more aware we become, through exercising better and better decisions.

Control, in this sense, isn't just about having power through the means of authority, status or money. The control we must focus on is about having a greater sense of security in knowing that the decisions we are making are the right ones to get us to where we want to be. Control is the map, guiding the ship, not the wind in its sails. Both are completely necessary for the journey to be successful but without the map, we are adrift and could end up anywhere! Imagine the sense of control of having significantly raised those odds in favor of achieving your destination, of having the ability to sift through all the choices you are going to make with a fine-toothed thinking comb that will give you just that ability and that confidence. When we look at the Tension Differential Factor we can see the difference between where we are and where we want to be. The control that we will be learning to exercise will be the sense of control felt through knowing that the skills we will be applying to reach our destination will greatly improve our chance of getting there, unharmed, full of vigor and empowered to continue onwards to our next step of the journey.

Right, enough of the mariner's analogies…for the moment, at least…

The Tension Differential Factor model illustrates a very important concept, namely, that there is always a gap between where we are and where we want or need to be. Now, to some people, this is a source of constant frustration. They look at the model and see only gloom and doom, threat and hopelessness, thinking that, no matter what they do, it will never be enough. They throw up their hands in despair and walk away from life.

There is another, more positive and constructive way to view the gap, however, and that is to see it as a source of constant challenge and opportunity, always stretching our potential capability one more notch. They see it as a chance for continuous improvement in whatever conditions or situation they find themselves. It is all a matter of perception, but what a difference it makes! It is this latter attitude that is constructive and creative.

The even better news is that we will always have the opportunities to develop and grow, plus the skills to do so within the framework of Transformational Thinking. It provides us not only with the map that permits us to explore new oceans of opportunity (sorry, couldn't resist it), but the skills that allow us to do so with broadened perspective so that we may identify those opportunities that exist. That is why we have called this section "*We hope you will **never** be all you can be*". This is a sincere wish. Our potential is unlimited. Whatever our personal circumstances, wherever we may be in the world, we *can* improve our lot in life. Sometimes that improvement will be small, sometimes even imperceptibly so to the outside observer, but as soon as the change is achieved, even as it is being attempted, the gap on the Tension Differential Factor shifts, and it shifts upwards. It will never stop shifting upwards. It must not. Every little perception we can improve, every little success that we achieve through applying new skills, every little drip of control we can eek out of our lives, all raise our bar of potential and new goals emerge.

Therefore, I reiterate: never be all that you can be. Never stop growing.

The Seven Stages of Change

Let's take a look at the process of change itself. There are seven stages, which can be broken down into three categories.

Conceptualization (Insight)

I must first perceive the need for and benefit of change. *(Perception)*

I must believe that I can change. *(Potential)*

I must establish clearly-defined goals. *(Purpose)*

Actualization (Action)

I must focus all my personal power in attainment of those goals. *(Intention)*

Reinforcement (Final Internalization)

I must recognize and celebrate my achievements. *(Reinforcement)*

I must share what I have learned with others. *(Inclusion)*

I must look for the next opportunity to expand, develop and grow. *(Expansion)*

Firstly, we gain the insight that tells us that change is possible and beneficial. We also believe we possess the personal perception, potential, and power to attain whatever goals we establish. We establish our plans, in accordance with our purpose(s).

Secondly, we set about making those plans come to life, using whatever resources are available. It is the actualization part of this process that transforms perception into reality, as we create the situation we desire.

Finally, there is reinforcement of our original belief, thinking and actions by way of recognition, celebration and sharing what we have learned with others. It is amazing to me how often this entire part of the sequence is omitted. How often do we achieve something, perhaps even a major victory, and do not spend the time to process what we have gained from the experience, choosing, instead, to set more goals?

The sharing of the knowledge we have attained is an important part of this step, though few of us make a conscious effort to do so. There are two major reasons for sharing the benefit of our experiences:

We reinforce our own learning. When you are able to share or teach something to someone else, you know that you have internalized the experience. One cannot impart that which one does not possess.

We gain the benefit of other people's input, insights and perception on the event, adding to the knowledge we have personally gained.

It is this last stage that prepares us for moving on to the next stage and further reinforces our thinking that we are on the right track. For the sharing of our experiences, by including and involving others, helps us attain the support we need to continue on indefinitely. Note, however, that we are not talking about boasting of our achievements; we are talking about co-processing it with others with whom we have established a bond of mutual trust and respect.

It is for this reason that I build ample time for sharing into the training and development programs that I design. In this Transformational Thinking program, for instance, there will be ample time to share and internalize what you are learning as you work through the course. This is why each new skill comes with a Personal Action Plan that encourages the behavior of practice, sharing and teaching what you have learned with others. During group sessions that I teach, the class will often spend the entire session just talking about the experiences they have encountered during the week, as a result of their Personal Action Plans. The amount of insight and interaction we achieve is always incredible. It is always time well spent. The schedule becomes secondary to the sense of discovery and adventure, as each person shares their newly gained insights and listens to the input of others.

In one session, three of the group on that day had actually changed jobs during the previous week. This was a result of coming to the conclusions that, for whatever reasons, they were unhappy with their current situations, applying some of the Lateral Thinking skills, as well as others I had taught them, such as networking their own realized potential, and gotten better positions. We also spent some time analyzing the methods used by a couple in the group and they saw the benefit of applying the skills they had learned to prevent a lot of conflict through better communication techniques and some of the other skills they had learned and which you will learn during the Politics section. Still another young man expressed how these sessions had helped him in dealing with some particularly difficult personal situations, remarking that this had come along at just the right time in his life.

This form of final internalization is a vital element in the process of Transformational Thinking. Those people we gather around us as our friends and family, will play a pivotal role in cementing our journey towards our purpose(s). There will always be times when doubts set in. This is natural, but can be controlled. This is when we must refer to the 10th 'P', that of Perseverance. By sharing our experiences and teaching others the skills that we learn, we will develop commonalities with those people around us, which build the bridges of trust and respect and encourage our perseverance to flourish.

For my own part, there are many changes that are taking and have taken place in my life. I share them with the friends, family and this is why I share them with you, here in this book. It is this sharing and the ability and willingness to listen to the insights of others that establishes the nature of trust and respect among individuals within a group and that will enable you to persevere with turning your purposes into reality.

Changes are always going to keep coming at us, no matter how well we plan or how well we think we are prepared for them. By using the Transformational Thinking program many of the changes that previously used to come out of left field can be better anticipated and either avoided or turned into opportunities if we are properly equipped, mentally and spiritually, to do so. Those that do take us by surprise don't have the devastating and paralyzing impact they did before, once we are trained and developed to think quickly, understand how to handle them and assume our part of the responsibility for doing so.

This is the most important change of all, this transformation from Victims of Circumstance into Champions of Change. As we begin to realize and tap into the personal power we each possess, we begin to see that we are the ones creating many of the changes that used to baffle us and we are able to redirect our efforts towards changes that have positive results.

By developing our perceptive abilities, learning to recognize our potential and to recognize and create opportunity, suddenly we lose our fear and anxiety that used to accompany even the smallest of changes. It is precisely this stage of development that prepares us to live life with faith and courage, for isn't that exactly what faith is . . . the absence of fear? No two thoughts can occupy the mind at the same time. That is why I begin each day focusing on whatever sources of anxiety I may have, taking note of their cause, then letting them go, replacing them with positive thoughts and plans. It sets the entire tone of my day.

In other words, referring back to the Seven Stages of Change, my day begins with Conceptualization. The rest is merely stages two and three, those of Actualization and Expansion. But, in order to get to the point of Conceptualization, one needs to develop certain skills to deal with the ego side of the picture, eliminating the force of fear. We will get into how this is done later on.

All of the internal processes that we currently use to think, have been learnt through our experiences. They have become as much second nature to us as driving is to the experienced driver. The driver no longer needs to think of when to signal, how to change gear or which pedal is the clutch. The same is true for thinking. The problem with thinking is that we have become so used to the processes that we use that we don't even know what they are. They have become second nature to us too. When learning new thinking skills, we must use and practice them in the same way until we no longer even notice that we're doing it.. We have internalized them and it is simply the new way we think and believe, the resultant behavior producing much more desirable outcomes. That is what it means to be a Champion of Change. Transformational Thinking can get us there. It becomes a way of living one's life.

Decisions, Decisions, Decisions!

Autopilot

We are faced with thousands of decisions every single day. Most of them are made without a second thought - tying a shoe, for example, or the hundreds of minor ones made in the process of driving a car, or the many that we make in dealing with others. They are made on the subconscious level, as a result of previous experience and habit and our brain's autopilot kicks in. Imagine what it would be like if we had to stop and consider every single action throughout the course of a day? We would be literally forced into inaction, so a part of the mind takes over the seemingly trite or unimportant ones for us, leaving the rest of the mind to consider how we are going to handle the more important ones. That is an oversimplification of how the mind works, perhaps, but it will suit our purposes.

Another way to look at this process is that we have established, over time, systems for doing certain things and performing certain activities. I remember working on an assembly line in a factory during a couple of summers of my high school days. At first, I had to pay attention to every single little detail, until I got it down to a system. Before too long, I was turning out more pieces than was necessary, seemingly with less than half the effort, and found my mind was free to roam and think about other things. The same can be said of many activities that some people regard as work, but others see as a form of mental relaxation. Mowing the lawn, trimming weeds from a garden and a host of others.

I refer to such work as mindless, not in a derogatory sense, but from the aspect that, once you have established a system and the more accustomed you are to repeating that system, the less concentration is required.

We will soon get into the process of how we make decisions and I will present you with certain skills designed with that in mind. For the purposes of this chapter, however, I want to address those conscious decisions we make and our responsibility for their results. If we are to become true Champions of Change, it is incumbent upon us to realize the true nature of the personal power we possess, before we begin the program, in order to fully unleash and tap into that power. In order to accomplish this, I have another analogy for you. I call it The Pebble in the Pond. It is such a simple story, but one that really gets the point across. I suppose this is why I love such parables.

The Pebble in the Pond

A decision is like a pebble we toss into a quiet pond. The ripples that emanate from the center and travel outwards in 360 degrees, are the effects of our decision. As they flow outwards, they touch everything in their path. So it is with our choices and decisions. They affect everyone around us directly or indirectly. But the parable doesn't end there. What happens when the ripples reach those objects or the far shore? They immediately reverse their direction and return to the source. That is the part we would most often like to forget about, yet we have many expressions we use to express this concept like: "What goes around comes around;" or "You reap what you sow;" or "You get back what you put in." There are many others, but I am sure you get the point.

Usually when we use these expressions, we are assigning them to some-one else. How often do we stop and consider this "natural" law when making a decision ourselves? Too rarely, I would say. We have expressions for these occurrences, as well, such as: "If only I had put my brain in gear before engag-ing my mouth!" Or "I wish I hadn't said/done that!" Or "If only I had known then what I know now…!" The beat goes on.

That is why it is so important to consider the possible consequences and ramifications of what we say and do before we commit ourselves by our behavior. Once the pebble has left your hand, it is too late to stop the ripples, and, yes, I believe they do return to the source.

Earlier, I mentioned what Edward de Bono refers to as the Intelligence Trap. It bears repeating here, because most of us are victims of our own in-telligence at one time or another. He tells the story of The Expert. See if this doesn't ring a personal bell in your memory.

The Expert

Once there was a group of people that were in the habit of cutting off those heads that contained opinions different from the ones they were push-ing at the time. One day they brought along a cart to where they had the guillotine set up. In this cart were three people: a consumer, a businessman, and an "expert."

First, the consumer was put on the guillotine. The lever was pulled and down came the blade and jammed one inch above the consumer's head. The crowd was unanimous, "This was an act of God!" So they let the consumer free, and being a good consumer, he went away muttering about the poor quality of the equipment.

Next, they put the businessman on the guillotine. The lever was pulled and down came the blade and, once again, it jammed one inch above the businessman's head. Again the crowd cried out, "Set him free!" and they did. Being a good businessman, he went away with ideas for starting a guillotine repair service.

Finally, they were about to get the "expert," but he leapt up onto the platform and with a gleam in his eye, he said, "You know, if you would just tighten that screw there and this one here, you will find that the machine will work perfectly"…and, of course, it did! Logically, the "expert" was correct, but perhaps there was something inadequate about his perception of this situation.

Logic may often lead us to the correct conclusion, but it is one's overall perception of events that provide the wisdom necessary to arrive at better decisions as to how and when to apply that logic. The Lateral Thinking skills you will learn in this book will greatly assist you in achieving better overall perception and hopefully, avoid some of the "pain" of applying solely logical reasoning to situations that might require a little "extra" thinking!

'Mysterious' Thinking

There is an interesting exercise I utilize in my training and development sessions to make another point regarding how we arrive at and handle decisions. I call it the two-minute mystery and more recently, as they have become a little better known, they have been called "Lateral Thinking Questions". Even if you know this particular mystery, it is a worthwhile exercise to think it through, because it perfectly illustrates our traditional methods of thinking.

There are several of these two-minute mysteries that I use, usually averaging three per session that I teach. I give the group a mystery to solve and they have two minutes in which to do so. The method they use is to ask me questions, to which I can only reply "yes,"" no," or "it doesn't matter."

The following is an example:

Mary and Ken go out for the evening. When they arrive back home, they find that the door is locked, just the way they left it and there are no signs of a break in. Suzie is dead on the living room floor in a pool of water and surrounded by shards of broken glass. In the master bedroom, they find Tom sound asleep on the bed. What happened?

As people start to ask questions in their search for the solution, they ask all kinds of questions, such as:

Did Suzie commit suicide? (No.)

How old is Suzie? (It doesn't matter.)

Did Tom kill Suzie? (Yes, but how?)

Did she die from cuts from the broken glass? (No.)

Was the glass from a broken coffee table? (No.)

Are Tom and Suzie related? (No.)

Are either Tom or Suzie related to Ken and Mary? (No.)

Did Tom poison Suzie? (No.)

Is Tom dead also? (No.)

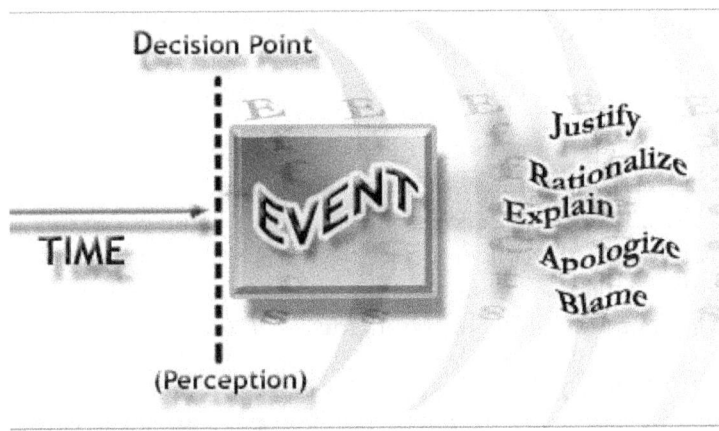

The questions go on and on. Sometimes, someone asks a question that gets everyone else thinking in a different direction, such as:

Are Tom and Suzie people? (No.)

Aha! You can see the wheels turning by this point. Sometimes they solve it; sometimes they do not. The answer is that Suzie is a goldfish and Tom is a cat. The rest is easy to figure out. The looks and sighs that follow are inevitable. As soon as you arrive at that conclusion, it is easy to solve the mystery. It appears so obvious in retrospect.

There are many of these out there and a number of excellent websites now dedicated to them. I have included a two-minute mystery on the title page of each of the Eleven P's of the program just for your fun and as an indication of how prone we can be to making assumptions when applying logical solutions to situations that may require just a little more "lateralized" thinking. For the answers you will need to visit the Transformational Thinking website or one of the many sites out there dedicated to these extraordinary and fun examples of how our perceptions can misguide us.

Back to the mystery. Why is it that so many people find it difficult to solve this and other little stories like it? Because they begin their line of thinking based upon the false assumption that Suzie and Tom are people. No matter how sound and logical their train of thinking from that point on, they are on the wrong track and headed in the wrong direction. And that is one of the flaws in logical, linear thinking. You have a logical starting point, and proceed in a linear manner from point to point until you reach the conclusion.

It doesn't matter whether they solve the mystery or not. That is not the purpose of the exercise. It is to show that we usually start our line of reasoning based upon the facts at hand, and our emotions and judgment at the beginning. This, more often than not, is the way many of us reach decisions.

The Traditional Decision-Making Process

In a real-world situation, as opposed to our two-minute mysteries, what is even more interesting is what follows after making that decision or reaching a conclusion. We now expend most of our time, energy, and effort trying to justify, defend, or develop the conclusion we have attained, rarely considering another possibility unless someone throws a signpost up, literally hitting us in the head to get our attention. Diagrammatically, it looks like this:

Our patterns of thinking directly and profoundly affect our reality. We literally create our own perception of reality by the way we view the world, based upon our unique individual logic bubble. A logic bubble is defined as the aggregate of all previous experience, attitude and emotion. This changes with our experiences and perceptions of them. So, our logic bubble will have a profound effect on our decision-making based upon our combined experience of the world at any given moment.

This means that, when we are faced with a situation, decision or event, we usually determine our reaction to the event according to the condition of our logic bubble at the time. At any given moment, a decision may be made based upon emotion, sentiment, or just downright greed, whatever the situation may be as determined by the bias of our logic bubble at the time. Very often, we will make a decision as to how we are going to handle the situation at first impact, or the moment when the event first occurs, then expend a great deal of time, energy and effort justifying our decision, should it be challenged. The effect of this is that once we have determined our opinion about something, we are most unlikely to change it and will probably defend it to the death rather than adapt our approach according to any new evidence that we are confronted by.

Just imagine, for example, if the second alien in our WW2 story had seen Oscar Schindler at work and simply denied that it was anything more than a blip of freakish behavior, completely unconnected with the true nature of human beings. His opinion, driven by the negative emotion he had whipped up after his brother's recollection of the murder and mayhem on Earth, could have caused him to deny the pertinence of his new information because it obviously contradicted the previous conclusion. He could have brushed it off as a "fluke", a mistake in his own observation of the facts, or even concluded that Oscar Schindler could not have been human because it contradicted the account of human behavior he had come to believe! And, believe it or not, this is very often how our decision-making process works because it is dogged by an almost neurotic need to be right in a decision-making environment that blames and shames anyone who is wrong! With this type of decision-making generally applied throughout the "Western" world, is it any wonder that we shake our heads at the quality of many of the decisions that are made around us? Moreover, why do we not sit back and question our own decision-making?

The mentality of decision-making we have internalized in the Western Culture is endemic and, should there be a better example of an internalized process in operation, I would very much like to see it, because it would make a wonderful addition to this book! The condition of our logic bubble, depending upon emotions or sentiments at any given time, the resulting decision and the subsequent defense of the decision at all costs, is an unreliable and dangerous way to go about life. In this regard, we are a dangerous bunch, ready to fire off opinions, decisions and perceptions on a whim, without much regard for the basis of them or their place in the greater reality of things.

Therefore, our judgment and emotion at any given moment, appears to have a great impact on the quality of any decision we may make. Also, the resulting mentality we have adopted with regard to shaming and blaming, explains the need to justify bad decisions at all costs, so that we are not shamed and blamed ourselves. The conclusion is that if we can suspend judgment and emotion until we are a little deeper into the event, or until we have gathered enough pertinent and relevant information to have an improved perception of the reality of the situation, we stand a much better chance of making a better decision. If we can internalize thinking skills that allow us to gather as many factors to consider prior to committing to a decision then it is much more likely that the resulting effect of the decision will be positive.

The main points in this section are as follows: If we can…

Gather as much information as possible from as many sources as possible then

Consider the information without judgment and emotion

and

Finally make a decision based upon this information

We are far more likely to make a better decision and thereby improve our reality and that of those around us.

And that is what Lateral Thinking is all about…making better decisions.

Note also that, liking an idea can lead us to a wrong conclusion just as easily as not liking an idea. Both are forms of prejudice that can lead us to incorrect solutions, or at least to ones not as beneficial as we can attain with an open mind through temporary suspension of emotion and judgment. And this is the point. We must strive for improvement, not perfection. Improved decision-making, improved thinking, improved perceptions: this is the goal and in each case the improvement must be constant and unwavering as we must all challenge the legitimacy and worthiness of every belief at each stage in our development. The great delusion is that something is the best. As I have pointed out and will continue to stress, Transformational Thinking is here to be improved upon too. It is the framework and the gateway to start people off. Just as Transformational Thinking will improve your reality should you choose to internalize its philosophy, so it will be improved upon by those that make the connections further down the road. This is an endless journey, folks. The Tension Differential Factor works for Transformational Thinking too!

Again, I will provide you with these Lateral Thinking skills to help us avoid these common thinking traps in the section on Perception.

Personal Choice is Personal Reality

There is one other important issue concerning decisions that we need to examine before continuing, however, and that is the freedom of choice we all possess when it comes to making choices and decisions.

How often have we said, "That person/situation makes me angry!" Is that really the case? Or is that a way of placing the responsibility for our own feelings and the resultant consequences of our decisions made in such a frame of mind, outside of ourselves, where it doesn't belong? Is it, in other words, just a cop out? Before you answer that, consider the following:

Contrary to accepted theory, seeing is not believing. Believing is seeing. We create our own reality through our perception. Think of the importance of that statement! You have choices. We make all decisions based upon how we perceive the situation. If we are living in a personal reality that is uncomfortable or unrewarding, we have the personal power to change it. It all begins in the mind with a thought, one's perception, and the decision to do so.

I cannot remember who said it and will leave it up to the quote specialists out there to look it up but I feel I should paraphrase this quotation: What we believe to be true, is true, or will become true. This is the nature of the concept that "Believing is Seeing". It is in the human mind that truth becomes reality and it is not always subject to any fact or plausible reasoning. We have the ability to believe something simply because we want to, devoid of any evidence to support it or in ignorance of any evidence to disprove it. In fact, it is sad to admit, as human beings, that, more often than not we tend to err on the side of this unfortunate natural tendency. Once we have formed an opinion about something in our minds, we internalize it as truth. I have mentioned before and make no apologies for the repetition, challenge everything. There is no truth that cannot withstand the light of challenge, only fabrication and lies will wilt under the assault of a thorough and strict analysis of challenge. So it is in each of our minds. As we believe it to be true, so we will see it as true, time and time again, despite and to the contrary of evidence that may disprove it.

When we apply this concept to our own feelings and emotions, we can see how we are misguided and our perceptions are "sold short" by concluding a form of response that returns to the Victims of Circumstance mind-set. There are many people who choose not to accept this as fact. Why? Because it is much easier to blame other people, situations, events, society, whatever, outside ourselves for our condition. Accepting the fact that our decisions and choices contributed to the situation, good or bad, means having to assume the responsibility for our own happiness. That means personal responsibility. It is considered by some to be preferable to remain "Victims of Circumstance," rather than taking on the responsibility involved in an increased awareness, and becoming "Champions of Change" by challenging the fact that we hand over control of our emotions day in, day out, often to complete strangers, because we simply cannot give up the lame excuse that we believe what we see.

Why relinquish control of your happiness and self-fulfillment to the hands of other people? Who would willingly do such a thing? In many societies around the world, we claim the importance of the individual's freedom. It is the basis on which many countries were founded and built. Yet, every day, so many of us do exactly that! We relinquish the control of our lives to complete strangers! Think about it this way:

You are driving down the A1, on your way to work or perhaps school, in a really good frame of mind. Then, suddenly and without warning, a guy cuts you off. Right then and there is a point of personal decision. What choice do you make?

Many choose to get angry, maybe try to catch the person and do the same to him. Suddenly your entire mood and frame of mind (perception) has changed in a fraction of a second. You arrive at your destination and someone says, "Hi, Bill, how are you today?" They are met by a grumbling and rumbling of anger that you are now carrying with you. No matter what, you can't seem to shake the anger. It affects everything you say and do. It is like there is the dark, massive cloud of anger surrounding you. And it is all that guy's fault!

You have just given control of your life to that person, that complete stranger. You have done so by choosing to get angry and stay angry. That person is living in your head rent-free. As silly as that sounds, we do it all the time! Maybe it was an argument with your spouse, or one of your kids, or a friend.

What do you suppose happens to the guy who cut you off? Do you think that, once he arrives at his destination and someone asks how he is, that he grumbles and says, "I am having a terrible day! I just cut someone off on the A1?" Do you think that incident has destroyed his day? I doubt it very seriously. He just tools on down the road, completely oblivious that you have relinquished control of your reality to him. It is all a matter of choice.

Am I saying that you do not have the right to be angry? Of course not. Such an approach would be ridiculous! But, what is important here is what you do with it. As we learn in meditation, that feeling is real and it is a sane reaction. Take note of it and get on with creating a positive reality for yourself.

The point is that you believe you have a right to your reaction. You probably do. You believe you have earned the feeling. You probably have. You believe the guy who cut you up deserves the lingering wrath boiling inside you. Maybe he does.

But you don't.

Don't carry this stranger in your head and heart all day. Let it go! Your primary focus should be your state of mind. None of us can expect to attain positive results with a negative frame of mind. Once again, this belief that it is right and correct to carry these emotional missiles around with us is an internalized process that we have learned throughout our lives from everyone around us. In the resulting explosions, who gets hurt? Just the person who deserves it? Wrong! Everyone that comes anywhere near it gets hurt and, to reiterate once again, you, in particular, do not deserve it. It damages your state of mind and, most importantly, the ripples from the stone you've just thrown, will come back and haunt you. To extend the example of the car, a friend of mine will willingly admit that the cause of his one driving accident in 15 years of driving was because he was angry with his wife, who happened to be sitting beside him at the time! Who got hurt from his anger? He did, twice in fact, because the resulting fury from his wife extends the example even further than we might need to go!

Cannot the same be said of our relationships with other people whom we know? No one else pushes our buttons, getting a negative response, unless we choose to allow them to do so. My spouse/friend/boss/customer doesn't make me angry. I choose to get angry. It is my choice. It is my decision, my responsibility and, try as I might, I cannot lay it on them.

Conceptual Awareness

I cannot over stress the importance of not only understanding the concepts presented in this chapter, but accepting them and I mean really accepting them. Challenge them. Examine them. But, without an understanding of how the decision-making process works and accepting our share of the responsibility for the results of our decisions, any further discussion of the personal power one possesses is completely and utterly academic. Regardless of one's external conditions or circumstances, no one, and I mean no one, can control your mind without your permission.

One's personal life is all about the decisions one makes. If we can learn to make better decisions, better plans, establish better goals and arrive at better solutions, then the quality of one's life is bound to take a turn for the better. That is precisely what Transformational Thinking is designed to help us accomplish.

Not only can Transformational Thinking help one achieve a more positive state of awareness, it also provides you with the necessary tools and skills to begin to make the changes in your life that will lead to self-fulfillment. Again, I want to stress that it doesn't matter a whit where one is at when one begins the journey of Transformational Thinking. There is something here for everyone due to its universal design, its simple concepts and easily applied, yet effective skills.

Before we get into the system of Transformational Thinking itself, we need to consider one other necessary factor. This is the backdrop that provides the system with the life it needs. That factor is the human spirit. In the following chapter, we are going to be taking a look at what we mean by the human spirit, and how it applies to the philosophy of Transformational Thinking.

The Human Spirit

In the process of definition, it is just as important to understand what something is not as comprehending what it is. Otherwise, we leave too much room for misinterpretation. The Human Spirit is not about religion. It is important to stress that right off the bat. It is not about Christian, Buddhist, Jewish, Moslem, Hindu, Bahai, or New Age views. It is a simple breakdown of the attributes each of us possess as human beings, members of a common race. This point cannot be over emphasized.

I am highly conscious of the fact that using the word "spirit" in the philosophy of Transformational Thinking could be misinterpreted as a reference to the human soul. Whether one believes in the concept of human soul or not, it is irrelevant to this philosophy and I would not presume to try to influence that belief one way or another.

Furthermore, so many so-called religions are exclusive in their approach. There are set precepts and credos, tenets and professions of faith that are required. This concept of the Human Spirit, as you will find, is not in violation of any of the aforementioned religions, yet it is a part of all of them. In other words, the fundamentalist Christian will find nothing here that is contradictory to the teachings of Christ; nor will the Buddhist find anything here that is contradictory to the teaching of Gautama, the Muslim in the teachings of the Quran, etc.

The Human Spirit, as used within the context of Transformational Thinking, consists of twenty attributes that we all possess, in varying degrees, and certain ones become of primary importance, dependent upon various situations. But we all possess them. Learning to appreciate and understand them helps us to better appreciate and understand our own self worth, not to mention that of other people we meet in life. We begin to perceive other people as human beings, rather than human "doings." We see people for what they truly are, rather than classifying them according to what they are currently doing in life. It helps to take a lot of the influence of the ego out of the picture, replacing it with a genuine inclusive spirit.

I am aware that there are many ways of defining what it is that makes us human. This is just a raft we use in Transformational Thinking to accomplish the goal, which is a broader understanding and appreciation of our own capabilities and those of others. Just like all other approaches or aspects of Transformational Thinking, this is intended to be of a supplemental nature.

The Twenty Attributes of the Human Spirit

What follows is a breakdown of each of the twenty attributes we all possess. Once we have defined them, the next step is to use this information to appreciate our own commonalities, but also to see how we are each unique and special, according to the way the various attributes rise to the surface, priority wise, according to various situations. It is an easy step from there to understand that recognizing and celebrating the attributes of the Human Spirit will bring about positive results, while violating them will result in negative responses and reactions.

I see so much emphasis placed on "dealing with people" these days, whether it be in management philosophy or customer awareness courses, but rarely have I ever seen anyone clearly define what a "people" is. How can we expect to deal successfully and effectively with a person, when we haven't the slightest clue as to the nature of the person with whom we are supposed to be dealing? The Human Spirit provides us with that insight.

Once we have defined these twenty attributes, we will then provide an exercise that will enable you to determine which are your predominant ones. In fact, I have designed this exercise to include a group of people so that we can get an even better understanding of the complexity of the Human Spirit. It is one that I normally include in my training and development sessions, but I include it here, in its entirety, for the benefit of the reader. I suggest that, to get the full impact, you conduct this exercise with several persons who know you well and obtain their feedback and perceptions. It can be a most eye-opening experience.

The Human Spirit answers the question: What is a person?	
1. Self-Conscious Being	11. Visionary Being
2. Self-Determined Being	12. Worship Being
3. Propositional Being	13. Harmonious Being
4. Intelligent Being	14. Security Being
5. Emotional Being	15. Aesthetic Being
6. Social Being	16. Trust Being
7. Physical Being	17. Love Being
8. Purpose Being	18. Leisure Being
9. Plan Being	19. Intuitive Being
10. Principle Being	20. Creative Being

When we are dealing with a single individual, regardless of how we may feel toward that person, we are dealing with every detail of every attribute above. It is a most remarkable collection of systems and resultant needs, behaviors, experiences and perceptions, which form the very essence of what we refer to as the "HUMAN BE-ING!"

Each of the attributes can be broken down further. Each carries with it resultant needs. There is a definitive, resultant, positive behavior when we approach the individual attributes in a celebratory manner, recognizing and fulfilling those needs. There is a very different and negative resultant behavior evoked when we approach the person in a disrespectful and discounting manner. This complete study of the attributes of the Human Spirit encompasses an entire book, and has taken years of research and study. We shall summarize here:

Attributes	Corresponding Needs
Self-Conscious Being	Recognition
Self-Determined Being	Involvement
Propositional Being	Explanation
Intelligent Being	Logic
Emotional Being	Support
Social Being	Inclusion
Physical Being	Space
Purpose Being	Reason
Plan Being	Direction
Principle Being	Honesty
Visionary Being	Challenge
Worship Being	Faith
Harmonious Being	Balance
Security Being	Safety
Aesthetic Being	Cleanliness
Trust Being	Openness
Love Being	Respect
Leisure Being	Time
Intuitive Being	Trust
Creative Being	Freedom

The next time you are in the presence of another human being, think of the full measure of their "Essence Of Beingness." You may find a higher level of respect and regard for them.

Now that we have learned the twenty attributes of the Human Spirit, it is time to examine them at a closer level in order to ascertain a better and more complete understanding of their nature. Just as a science course teaches you the essence and nature of the basic elements so you can determine the interactive results of mixing them, so this course will show you the essence of human chemistry. We have broken the Human Spirit down into its basic elements. Now let us explore each and learn the true nature of each.

1.   Self-Conscious Being

The Self-Conscious Being is aware of itself. It communes with itself. There is always self-talk taking place. This attribute accounts for our self-awareness and self-contemplation. It leads us in our quest for self-fulfillment. It permits us to form images of ourselves, reflect upon our internal nature and esteem ourselves. This is the attribute that knows, intuitively, that "I exist and have meaning and significance."

2.   Self-Determined Being

The Self-Determined Being is volitional, possessing the power and freedom to choose. It is very conscious of the act of choice and cherishes it. It is self-governing and autonomous and resents outside interference with individual liberty and freedom. Within this attribute lies free will.

3.   Propositional Being

The attribute of the Propositional Being is responsible for our fascination with and love of language theory, conceptual thinking ability, all spelling, reading and writing. It constantly seeks symbols and responds to metaphorical examples. It drives us to preserve our history and information, always seeking to link us in time to the past and the future. It also loves semantics, naming, defining, labeling, explaining, and all forms of communication. It deals in representational systems and has an immense propensity for mathematics and numbers. It is always seeking knowledge, desires exactness and strives for continual learning.

4.   Intelligent Being

The Intelligent Being attribute is predominantly represented by the left-side of the brain. It deals in logic and reason, concepts and principles. At the same time, it deals very well with generalizations, classifications and inference. It loves knowledge and thrives on analytical thinking. It is the seat of synthesis, wisdom, evaluation, memory, comprehension and interpretation. We rely on it for quantifying, measuring and accuracy.

5.   Emotional Being

The Emotional Being is affective, showing all emotions and feelings. It reflects anger, passion, hate, love, humor, happiness, excitement, loneliness, sadness, gratitude and fear. It is very closely allied with the Creative and

Social attributes.

6. Social Being

This is the relational attribute. The Social Being needs bonding, companionship and love. It is communicative and trusting in nature. It is that part of us that reaches out to others and gives, as well as receives. It is the basis of appreciation and gratitude.

7. Physical Being

The Physical Being attribute is the bonding of body/mind/spirit. It provides our sense of personal space and also provides the responses to our five senses of touch, smell, sight, sound and taste. It is the kinesthetic part of us in which we find our motor skills. It is that part of us that provides a sense of being in place.

8. Purpose Being

The Purpose attribute of our Being is one of the earliest awakening of awareness. One of the first questions we ask (and never stop asking) is, "WHY?" The Purpose Being attribute establishes causes and supports them freely. It establishes relevance and identity. It needs to know that what we are and needs to feel that what we do, has significance and meaning.

9. Plan Being

The Plan Being attribute is that part of us that projects into the future, providing a vital link between where we are and where we want to be. It is future and time oriented. It is also aware of the past and provides the internal link in space and time. It is goal and purpose driven, organizational and strategic. It loves to design and manage. It is methodical and calculating. It relishes technique and implementation. It is the actualizing attribute of the person.

10. Principle Being

The Principle Being attribute provides our intuitive sense of right and wrong. It is the "belly barometer." It feels guilt and shame, feels responsible and accountable. It is the basis for character and moral conscience. It is the law maker and creed maker. It provides our internal code of ethics and moral values.

11. Visionary Being

Where would we be without the Visionary Being attribute? It is this attribute that provides our dreams and fantasies. It is the designer within us, the tool maker, the design and tool user. It establishes high expectations and seeks to meet them. It is the seat of our ambition and responsiveness to challenge. It is the goal setter and adventurer.

12. Worship Being

It is the Worship Being that provides us with our propensity to worship and gives us a sense of a higher power and purpose. It is our God-consciousness, providing for the establishment of 360 faiths and eleven major religions. It is the basis for our need for mythology and mystery. It is founded in a deep inner faith. It thrives on grace, forgiveness, love and patience.

13. Harmonious Being

The Harmonious Being attribute provides us with the need for balance and harmony, being one of the strongest driving natural attributes we possess. It likes structure, alignment, congruence and accord. It needs moderation, established boundaries and symmetry in all things.

14. Security Being

The Security Being attribute is one of the most basic of all human attributes. It requires safety and freedom from threat or danger. It is the basis for survival. It is the "fight or flight" attribute, needing basics such as sustenance and shelter. This attribute is also the basis for our adaptability and response to change, both external and internal.

15. Aesthetic Being

The Aesthetic Being is that part of us which is perceptive and appreciates beauty and grace, elegance and refinement. It likes culture, proportion, balance, form, orderliness and cleanliness. The Aesthetic Being has strong moral sensibility. But it also possesses that sense of awe, that spirit of adventure one experiences when watching a sunset.

16. Trust Being

The Trust Being attribute is that part of us which harbors belief, values, faith, confidence, dependability, authenticity, commitment and reliability. We want and need to trust and be trusted. It sets high expectations and is the basis for all meaningful relationships, along with respect.

17. Love Being

The Love Being is that part of us that requires companionship, relationships, personal commitments, affection, devotion, passion, tenderness and bonding. It needs to know that there is value and worth in a relationship. It demands consideration and nurturing. It is that part of us that continually seeks to give more than it receives. It is the primary driving force for many people.

18. Leisure Being

This is probably the one attribute we all wish we had more of! The Leisure Being likes ease and calm, prefers to be undisturbed and likes to be entertained and amused. It is fun loving and relishes games. It is very much in tune to the creative attribute. It also strives for convenience and simplicity.

19. Intuitive Being

This is the part of us that loves to play with ideas, concepts, plans and designs. It is predominantly a right-brained attribute, which follows hunches, trusts gut feelings and goes far beyond logic and reason. It is the seat of our imagination and the part of us that loves lateral thinking. It allows us to visualize and project. It is the source of all ideation and perception.

20. Creative Being

The Creative Being is the inventor, the artist, the poet, the musician, the discoverer and adventurer. It is this attribute which provides us with imagination, reason, ambiguity and metaphor. It loves problem solving, theorizing, hypothesizing, laterally thinking and ideation. It is inquisitive and questioning. It is horizon-expanding. It loves to marvel and wonder, and has a fascination for the unknown, always seeking new challenges.

That is a description of each of the attributes. Remember, we all possess all twenty in varying degrees, some being more predominant than others. Becoming adept at recognizing the predominant attributes in any individual provides one with the information required to deal with that person most effectively.

But, as in most cases, this knowledge begins with the knowledge of one's self. The better I understand my own nature, the better I am able to change that which I need to develop (character defects and weaknesses), and the better I am able to capitalize on my particular predominant attributes (character strengths). Survival is best utilizing our individual strengths; success is best developing our weaknesses.

Authenticity vs. Artificiality

Let us first take a look at each attribute from the point of view of a differentiation between Authenticity and Artificiality. We have all known persons that seemed so authentic. We often describe them as "real people." On the other hand, we have also known many people who are artificial. We often describe them as "plastic."

People who are authentic are to be trusted and respected. Those who are artificial are not. Both authenticity and artificiality stem from the same attributes. One could describe them as being at opposite ends of the spectrum.

When we are operating from a base of human spirit, we are in the authentic mode. When we are operating from a position of ego, we are in the artificial mode. If we are performing a proper in-depth self-analysis, we will find certain areas in which our internal pendulum swings at certain times, under certain circumstances, toward the side of authenticity. At other times, in other circumstances, we will discover we are leaning more toward the artificial end of the spectrum. Remembering that no one has yet achieved perfection, and that there is always room for improvement (The Tension Differential Factor), we all have areas which could use some attention that can be identified by a little bit of good, honest introspection.

Introspection or self-inventory is a healthy practice. It is a skill which should be performed regularly and consistently, just like preventative maintenance on one's automobile. Unfortunately, many of us have never learned how. The following exercises are designed to accomplish just that purpose. Examine the check sheet on the following page and then follow the procedures presented after. It is a quick and simple process, which tells one exactly where one exists on the scale.

Please note, self-inventory is not intended to be a practice in self-flagellation. The purpose is not to depress oneself. It is to illuminate those areas of strength and weakness we all, as human beings, possess. A proper approach dictates total honesty, not false humility or pride. If you are sincere about wanting to constantly improve and progress on the journey of life, accurate information is the key. It is to that purpose and end we offer this exercise. Like all others, it should be approached with a balance of fun and sincerity.

As we discussed in the previous section on decision-making, take care to suspend undue emotion and judgment. Reach deep inside and turn on the lights. The result of better understanding of one's internal issues is the ability to develop clear goals and plans for improvement. This is based entirely on your view of yourself, not other people's. Leave other people's point of view out of the process for the moment. There will be plenty of time for that later. I have never discovered too many people who are reluctant to tell me what they think of me when asked. It's the old line, "If you don't want to know the answer, don't ask the question."

The Authenticity / Artificiality Comparison of Human Spirit

Attribute	Authenticity	Artificiality
Self-Conscious	Spirit-Driven	Ego-Driven
Self-Determined	Tenacious	Stubborn
Propositional	Knowledge-Seeking	Manipulative
Intelligent	Systems Thinker	Critical
Emotional	Open / Caring	Angry
Social	Bonds Well	Controlling
Physical	Secure in Self	Overbearing
Purpose	Higher than Self	Self-centered
Plan	Strategic	Worry/Fear
Principle	Strong Internal Moral Code	External Code of Convenience
Visionary	Seeks Challenge, Plans Approach	Dream and Fantasizes
Worship	Humility	Self-Inflated Pride
Harmonious	Seeks Balance	Overindulgent
Security	Secure in Faith	Insecure in Fear
Aesthetic	Sense of Awe	Easily Bored
Trust	Transparent / Open	Closed Mind
Love	Giver	Take / User
Leisure	Uses Free Time Creatively	Wastes Time
Intuitive	Trusts Self and Intuition	Needs External Validation
Creative	Constructive	Destructive

An increased awareness of the resultant needs and corresponding behaviors that can be expected by authentic or celebratory approach versus artificial or violating approach can make a tremendous difference in the responses and resultant behaviors in any person with whom we interact.

For instance, when you have an entire organization in which everyone is aware of the attributes of the Human Spirit, there is no longer any excuse for violations, regardless of level of command. Everyone is responsible, as increased awareness brings with it a proportionate increase in responsibility. Once we are both aware, and I violate an attribute of your Human Spirit, it is not only your right . . . it is your responsibility to bring the violation to my attention.

Note that celebratory approaches will bring about positive resultant behavior, whereas violations will cause negative response. All too often, we receive a response that is totally unexpected. We need to examine our approach. Did we either inadvertently or by purposeful design violate the other person's Human Spirit? Whether intentional or unintentional, we are still responsible for our own behavior and words, as well as the consequences.

At present, we are looking at the Human Spirit in terms of our personal situation and hoping that we can take some steps to work on our deficiencies and develop further our strengths. This is part of our strategy of working from the inside-out. However, I have used an organization as an example above and can promise you that I have encountered incredible responses from companies all over the world that have taken this approach.

Just imagine for a moment, a whole country adopting the approach! Rather than looking at this point of the Visionary attribute as a dream (artificial), maybe we should look at it as the challenge to plan our approach (authentic)! This isn't some dream, it really works and this is the departure point for the rest of this journey. By looking at ourselves, our own behaviors, tempering them with respect of others and working to build trust, we can change our whole environment and adapt our personal realities. Now, with increased awareness of the human spirit that is integral in every human being, we can see where differences of opinion or perception of other people can be avoided with a little more understanding of what makes people "tick". The resultant benefits to a person adopting this strategy are improved trust, respect and perception of others and a better quality of interaction with people in general. Within a group, the effect is multiplied by the members adopting the same attitudes, the same respect and the same trust of those people that they can rely upon not to violate their human spirit. Taking this further, expanding it outwards to encompass everyone that we meet, it is easy to see how huge the impact could be.

We're starting small, focusing inwards, perceiving the opportunities to celebrate the human spirit in all those around us in order that, even those who have no knowledge of human spirit, can benefit indirectly from our awareness of it. The journey, underway and in full swing, begins from the celebration of this human spirit in each and every one of us.

Get on board!

One-On-One Celebration Of The Human Spirit Exercise

Purposes: To identify the Human Spirit Attributes in ourselves

To identify those attributes in others as we perceive them.

To compare our perceptions with others

Procedures: This exercise can be done in a group or alone, but it is better if done in a group. Believe it or not, in your group, you do not have to know each other all that well for this exercise to work. It is based more upon intuition than logical, in-depth character and personality studies.

Step One: In the space provided, from the list of twenty attributes, list the five predominant attributes of your Human Spirit as you perceive yourself. What are your five most obvious character traits? (Do not over-think this exercise. Go with your gut responses.)

My Five Most Predominant Attributes:
1.
2.
3.
4.
5.

Step Two: Prioritize them below (on the left) in order of what you consider to be the ones most important or predominant (#1), in descending order to the least predominant (#5). (Leave the column to your right blank for the moment. That will be filled in after the next two steps.)

	My Self-Perception	Others' Perceptions
1.		
2.		
3.		
4.		
5.		

Step Three: If you have managed to get together in a group, consider the other members of the group, one-by-one. Indicate what you consider to be their Single Most Predominant Attribute. If you are doing this alone, think of some people close to you who you think would not object to doing this exercise and perform the same task. Later on you can go to them and get them to fill in the other parts.

	Person's Name	Predominate Attribute
1		
2.		
3.		
4.		

5.		
6.		

Step Four: Seek the input from your team members and list them in the right-hand column back in Step Two. Compare the results.

Feedback

Note that each of us has many "selves".

1. The <u>real</u> self. This is the "me" that exists beneath all the layers of the personality onion. There are many people who do not perceive that part of themselves at all. A typical example would be the individual who has a low self-esteem. That person is blind to his or her true capabilities.

2. The <u>self-perceived</u> self. As in the above example, the person with a low self-esteem sees himself as a failure. On the opposite end of the spectrum, we have the egocentric person who has an inflated sense of self. Most of us are somewhere in the middle.

3. The self as <u>perceived by others</u>. There can be as many versions as the number of individual perceptions we are dealing with at any given time.

Also, being adaptable creatures, different attributes will surface and dominate according to the needs and demands of the situation. For example, right now, my survival instinct is pretty much in the background, but if a truck were to come rolling through the wall, that self would come to the forefront rapidly and become the predominate self until the perceived danger was passed.

Learning to recognize the various attributes of the Human Spirit is a great aid in recognizing our own potential and that of others. This is where true and sincere recognition begins.

If you will notice, I stressed the importance of relying on intuition during this exercise. There is an important reason for that, not the least of which being that intuition is exactly what we use every time we are introduced to a stranger or walk into a room of people we have never met before. We need to begin listening to our intuitive selves more often. Most women are better at it than most men. It is part of their genetic structure, I suppose.

But we also have to temper that intuition with an open mind. Forming an opinion based upon intuition alone can be just as dangerous and wrong as not doing so at all. It is a delicate balancing act which most of us need to work on.

Having an appreciation of the twenty attributes of the Human Spirit can greatly benefit us in this endeavor, since it provides us with a mental check sheet, containing all positives and no negatives. Imagine the difference this respect for others and actively seeking their attributes rather than their flaws can make in relationships, whether they be of a personal or a professional nature!

One of the things that this list has done for myself and for many to whom I have taught it, is to make them much more sensitive and aware of the nature of others. I look upon every human being I meet today as being someone from whom I can learn. I am not so much interested in what they do for a living as who and what they are as human beings. I look for the attributes of their Human Spirit.

Another dimension added to our understanding is that of Artificiality and Authenticity. Understanding that both are founded in the same attributes does not mean that some people are intrinsically bad, while others are innately good. They are simply manifestations of the same attribute at different ends of the spectrum, one end represented by the ego and the other represented by the spirit. This assists us in doing away with the judgmental approach we so often use. For to do so is ego based. Remember I said earlier that, as we attain more and more spiritual awareness, the need for judgment and emotion becomes less and less a part of the decision-making process? That extends to our relationships with other people too.

What I have presented here, in this section on the Human Spirit, is just the tip of the iceberg. There is a lot more to it, but I felt that this basic treatment of the subject is adequate to provide us with the backdrop we need to see how the philosophy of Transformational Thinking coincides with the appreciation and awareness of the Human Spirit.

The entire study of the Human Spirit contains enough material for another book, as we begin to examine how each attribute's needs result in different behavior, depending upon the way they are approached. There are many exercises to assist us in determining the impact these attributes have upon us and the people around us, but that depth of information and knowledge is not "need-to-know" information for our purposes. Simply a basic understanding is all we need.

This basic understanding is sufficient to establish the foundation we need to begin thinking in terms of mutual trust and respect, so necessary for any healthy human relationship. Armed with this knowledge, we can look at people from a slightly higher vantage point, seeking the goodness in them, rather than looking for and concentrating all our attention on their weaknesses, which we all possess in one degree or another. In other words, none of us have attained perfection yet. It is not so much a question of "right or wrong," just different attributes in different priorities.

Mutual trust and respect are integral in the process of Transformational Thinking. When we use the Twenty Attributes of the Human Spirit, we are not doing so in order to get some cynical advantage over others who are not using it. It will help us with our interaction with others and lead us towards a better sense of respect for who they are. Trust, the partner of respect, comes through consistently applying honesty and principles. Don't forget, a loss of trust, although implying a loss of respect, does not have to be that way. As we have already covered, you do not have to trust someone to respect them as human beings. A lack of respect is as much a signal of our own violation of the human spirit as it is a sign of what someone else may have done to you. If all else fails, as we will come to in a later chapter, the influence that may be doing you harm can be removed from the equation all together. It is all a matter of choice. You don't have to be a victim.

It is important that we all learn to curb our tendency towards judgment of others and ourselves. Such a tolerance is what leads to an open mind and an open mind is one that has both the capability and the capacity to learn. A closed mind does not. As a Greek philosopher once said, "You cannot teach that to a man which he thinks he already knows." We must open our minds, challenge what we think to be true until we can take it on board. Even then, it should not stay on board as a free-loader. It must continually pass the test of challenge and if it fails, it must be developed or replaced with something better. In the broad spectrum of people that we meet, the principle is the same. We must challenge our assumptions of people and see them for what they really are. This is self-development focusing on our perceptions of people through their human spirit. We start with ourselves and begin to behave in a way that we would like everyone to treat us. With trust and respect. If everyone does it, we will soon see what a difference a little thinking can make!

Summary of The Journey So Far

So far, in the Transformational Thinking system we have looked at a number of basic principles, concepts and skills that will be vital tools for the journey before us:

The concept of "change"

The seven stages of change

The importance of perceptions to us

The Tension Differential Factor (Potential)

The decision-making process

An introduction to lateral thinking

Freedom of choice

The concept of "Human Spirit"

Throughout the introduction and all through this explanation of the basic concepts of the system, I have stated that we each possess the personal power to change our reality. The concepts that have been presented thus far are fairly basic ones that set the foundation for the philosophy of Transformational Thinking. They are based upon certain assumptions which I have challenged, and which I certainly hope you have been challenging as we progressed through them. Is it important that you accept every single one of them? Not at all. Remember that the purpose of Transformational Thinking is not to convince you away from assumptions you currently hold or choose to believe in; its purpose is to supplement them.

I always refer back to the parable of the raft. If they assist you in the attainment of your goals, then use them. If and when they become a burden to you, discard them and continue on your journey unburdened. The same holds true, at least in my experience, with all assumptions. There are those that assist us in making our reality a better quality; there are others that impede our spiritual progress; there are still others that are absolutely detrimental to our spiritual well-being.

Only each individual can select and choose the raft appropriate for their own journey. What I am presenting here has worked for me, and I started much further from the path than most. These concepts have also worked for countless people with whom I have shared them. The only determining factor is whether or not you feel that they can help you. If they can, then, by all means, take them, incorporate them and pass them along.

It is important to stress another factor before making that final determination, however, and that is the suspension of emotion or judgment until you have seen the entire philosophy of Transformational Thinking, as a whole. All we have done so far is set the stage for what is to come. It was necessary for us to accomplish that, so that you have a good idea where we are headed and why.

These first few chapters have accomplished that purpose. We have studied the process of change, how it is achieved and what we are responsible for. We have looked at our decision-making process and how it is fundamentally flawed by our own assumptions and tendency to support the decision despite any evidence to the contrary. We have looked at the concept of Human Spirit, defining the twenty attributes that are within us all, in order that we might have a better understanding of the complex interactions between us. And we have gone deeper into a number of issues that need to be thought out before we progress to the program itself. These concepts are the foundation for what you will now learn. They act as guiding elements to the skills and thinking tools that will be described in the following chapters. As such, these principles act as the glue to which all the following will attach itself, piece by piece. That was the bread, if you will. Now it is time to put the meat in the sandwich and take a look at the philosophy of Transformational Thinking itself. However, at this point, I apologize wholeheartedly for that, and numerous other poor metaphors and can only stress that from here on in, they get worse.

Stay with it. How bad can they get...?

How does Transformational Thinking work? How can I apply it in the real world? How will it make my reality a better one? All these answers and more will be answered in the following chapters, as we move through the philosophy, step-by-step.

Let's just review the various steps of Transformational Thinking, in order to see where we are going by looking back at the meaning of the Eleven P's:

Perception

Potential

Principles

Passion

Politics

People

Purpose

Plans

Processes

Perseverance

Pliability

From now on, the Eleven P's will be our guide, starting with a topic we have already touched upon Number One: Perception.

TRANSFORMATIONAL THINKING: CHAMPIONS OF CHANGE

Part two

Firstly, as you progress through the remainder of this book, get into the habit of applying what you are reading to yourself, first and foremost. See how it applies to you as a person, and how you can apply it within your own reality, rather than directing that knowledge at other people outside yourself. If you have been able to accomplish that to this point, congratulations!

Another suggestion…one, in fact that I consider to be crucial to the process of Transformational Thinking…is putting what you learn into practice. For that reason, and in order to gain the most benefit from this book, I recommend taking occasional breaks and thinking about what you have read, then formulating a *Personal Action Plan* that will enable you to transform knowledge into action. This is the only way we can really and truly see if it works or not.

If you've never come across a Personal Action Plan before, the basic concept is that you write down what you're going to do, how you're going to do it and record your results. Don't worry, there are particular sections in which I have opted to include them. That is for the purposes of serving as a reminder and getting you into the habit of using them. Believe me, they are vital tools to maintaining your perseverance and recording the successes and interesting results you will achieve from here on in. However, there are other sections in which I have just as deliberately chosen not to include them so that you get accustomed to designing your own. A Personal Action Plan can be devised to process any new information or input we receive, regardless of the source. It consists of four parts:

Sit down and think about the input. Then write a paragraph or so describing what new insights or reinforcement of former concepts you may have held from the input.

Design an action plan that details how you intend to use this information, translating into the everyday application necessary to incorporate the knowledge internally, and so that it manifests itself in your life. How are you going to apply it? The more detailed this plan, including specific days, dates, times, people, etc., the more likely it will become a reality.

The third part is to go out there and do it, recording the results. If it didn't work the first time, consider why and revise your plan.

The final part of a personal action plan is to share the insights and experience with another human being, preferably one who is living and capable of response. The importance of this part of the process is so that we can reap the benefits of other people's perspectives.

Remember that Transformational Thinking is not intended just to be mental cannon fodder. Its real value only becomes evident when you translate the concepts and skills included within the philosophy into your life. The results are the proof of its worth, not just the claims of myself and others.

In terms of the length of time that this program should take you to complete, well, that is a personal issue. Some of the assignments and tasks I have included in the program are quick and easy whereas others require considerable introspection, thought and consideration. As the program is meant to be an interactive process, I would not imagine it possible to read it through in one sitting without incurring considerable loss of its desired effect. There is much within it that cannot reasonably be completed in minutes or hours. Some processes should last for the rest of your life, they are simply *that* indispensable and are flexible and changeable systems that accord with our ever-changing lives. Remember, this course is designed to assist you in a transformational process and that requires you to take as much time as necessary to thoroughly complete the task involved and formulate your own improved reality. We cannot expect to do that over a cup of coffee and a bagel. My advice is to progress at your own pace, digesting each chapter fully and completing each task to the best of your ability before moving on. That may take some time but the results will be far more rewarding than the reader who is bent on getting to the end in double-quick time.

Change, in this case, is a measured and calculated affair. You are committing to it by having made the choice to read this far. As we enter the program, you should proceed at your own pace and participate fully in each step. The measure of how well you are proceeding is your own gauge. From this point on, your gauge will be the positive effects that Transformational

Thinking will have upon your life.

Finally, before heading into the first chapter of the program, remember, this is supposed to be a journey of fulfillment and discovery, but most importantly, it's supposed to be fun! Enjoy what you learn, use what you feel is of value and experience what comes of it with a smile. Everything you benefit from should be celebrated and every improvement in your life enjoyed.

After all, that's what a great journey is meant to be about.

Part 2: *The System*

Two- Minute Mystery No. 1: The Elevator

A man lives on the 15th floor of n apartment block. Each day he leaves his apartment to go to work. He calls the elevator and, once inside, presses the ground floor button. When he returns from work he calls the elevator from the ground floor, enters the elevator and presses the 10th floor button. At the 10th floor he gets out of the elevator and walks the final 5 floors up to his apartment. Can you explain why?

Perception

Potential

Principles

Passion

Politics

People

Purpose

Plans

Processes

Perseverance

Pliability

CHAPTER FIVE

Perception

Expanding our Perceptions

Perception is a two-way street. It is not only how we view the world, projecting what we believe and how we think into our reality and that which surrounds us, it is also how we translate and process the information we receive. Obviously, two of the three systems I have previously described are the principle role players in this drama; namely the belief system and the thinking system. Though the two are closely related, all things being interconnected, so to speak, we are going to treat each as a separate, yet still connected entity. This simplifies the process.

Once we have dissected them, examined and improved each, we can easily reassemble them. We will deal with the belief system in the section on principles. For now, we are going to take a look at the way we think and examine three Lateral Thinking skills designed to improve and expand our perception.

I have mentioned several times that the philosophy of Transformational Thinking is inclusive and expansive, by nature and by design. It is interesting to me to dwell on that concept for a moment before we get into the key that unlocks the door to all future expansion . . . perspective.

As we become more aware through the application of Lateral Thinking, everything expands outwards. It just seems to grow and grow. We recognize more potential than we ever considered possible, both internal and external; we begin to adapt certain principles that include the needs and expectations of others; we discover interests and passion that are continuously refueled by more and more information and increased awareness; we begin to establish purposes and plans of which we previously might have thought we were incapable of attaining; we meet people, extending our networking potential out and out, since we are more open to the perceptions of others; our processes become more finely tuned and tweaked, always continually improving, albeit in incremental steps; our perseverance expands as we become more pliable in our thinking, which in turn, opens our perception even more; and so it goes on. Always evolving, ever expanding, taking us to new plateaus of understanding and achievement.

The key that unlocks that door is our perception. I suppose that accounts for my fascination with Dr. Edward de Bono and my admiration for what he has contributed to our culture through his Lateral Thinking. It adds an entirely new dimension to our mental sight, taking us farther than one lifetime should reasonably allow us to go. Although there are well over one hundred of his individual Lateral Thinking skills, each with its specific purpose, I have found three that are more than adequate to fuel the fires of an expanding mind for years to come. It is those three skills that I present to you here. I present them in the form of a workbook approach, so that you may progress through and savor each one; then learn the next, and so on. The beauty in Lateral Thinking is their interconnectedness. To any given situation, problem, event, decision, or whatever, you can apply one, two, or all three. No matter how you use them, the more you do so, the more rapid your growth as a thinker. What a thing to put on your resume! That is what we need more of in virtually every segment of our society . . . more creative and innovative thinkers. So, without further adieu, as they say, I present you with three perception expanders that are guaranteed to astonish your friends, curl your hair, straighten your teeth and make childbirth a pleasure. (Well, okay, so maybe that last line was a slight exaggeration.)

Burning Conclusions

Suppose I were to suggest to you that we go out and burn every book on logic we could lay our hands on? Most people would hear that idea and immediately make a decision, albeit subconsciously. They either like it, or they do not like it. They either approve or disapprove. The point is that they have made a decision without considering all the ramifications, consequences, or other possible solutions. As we looked at in the chapter "Decisions, Decisions, Decisions!" they are already committed and probably ready to defend their point-of-view. Whether you agree with the proposition or not, any snap decision you make at this point in the process is based upon emotion and judgment and can lead one to a false conclusion.

The key to clear thinking is simple in theory. We must learn how to temporarily suspend emotion and judgment. I say it is simple in theory because I can demonstrate it by suggesting that all taxi cabs should fly. Some people think, "Wow! That is a great idea," and they start thinking of and listing all the reasons that it is a good idea. Others will hear it and exclaim, "That is a bad idea," and they will begin to list all the reasons it won't work, providing barrier after barrier.

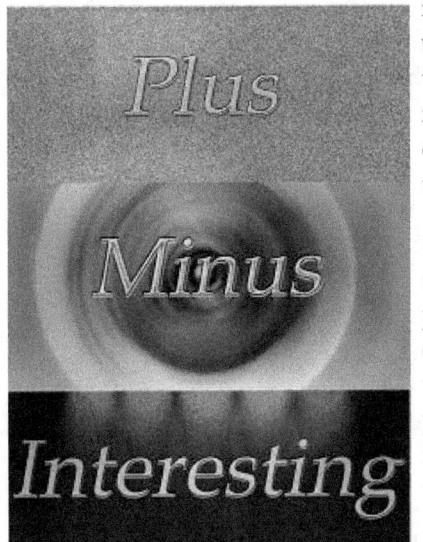

Both approaches are equally as dangerous. What has really occurred is that they have made their decisions up front, and now all their energy and time is spent proving to everyone else the reasoning behind their original decision, defending their position. And isn't that the way many of us debate and argue?

It is far better to suspend judgment and emotion until AFTER we have explored all possibilities, and not commit ourselves to this course of thinking or that before doing so. Yet, how many of us actually practice that simple tip? That is not the way we have been trained to think.

Now, it is simple to delay emotion and judgment when the situation or concept is a non-threatening one, like flying taxi cabs. It becomes more and more difficult to do so, the closer we come to our own prejudices, positive or negative . . . it doesn't matter which, for either one can still commit us to the wrong assumption and train of thought thereafter.

For example, take the debate on abortion or any other hot issue of our time. People tend to get really emotional about subjects that approach closer to our core belief systems. They get really defensive, and sometimes down-right offensive about the views they hold. That is why it is better to start practicing this skill with non-threatening situations or concepts.

Some people, when faced with a really serious decision, will make a list of the positives on one side and all the negatives on the other. But I guarantee you that, if they have not been made aware of the importance of suspending judgment and emotion, they will usually pepper the side they had originally wanted to go for in the first place. Take a decision like buying a car.

If you really want that car, you will find and list all kinds of reasons why it is a good idea and very few on the other side of the page. But, if your significant other disagrees with the wisdom in buying a new car, I can equally guarantee that the negative side of their page will be swarming with reasons to back up their point-of-view.

The first of the Lateral Thinking skills I am going to introduce to you not only helps us to balance both sides of the list of options and factors, it also adds a third dimension. It is this third dimension that is, to me, the most powerful aspect of this incredible tool, for it is in this "interesting" area, so rarely considered with equal attention, that we find the innovative and creative possibilities we probably would never have otherwise considered.

The PMI (Plus/Minus/Interesting)

The **PMI** is the deliberate focusing of one's full attention and energy equally to all sides of the issue without any preconceived notions or prejudice. For example, let's use this same idea, that of buying a new car.

Do not consider whether you like the idea or dislike it. The key to performing a successful PMI is to temporarily suspend judgment and emotion until after we have considered as many factors as possible. There will be plenty of time to commit to the idea later on. The key here is to realize that we are only playing with the idea for the time being. That's how one is better able to maintain that degree of non-commitment that is so crucial. This is a skill that we should not take too seriously. Get used to having fun with the thinking process!

Take three minutes and list as many factors as you can possibly come up with on the Plus side. Another key is not to judge your ideas. We are not interested in the quality of the ideas. We are going strictly for quantity. How many can you list in three minutes? Pluses only. The questions you should be asking are: Why is this a good idea? What is good about this idea? Why would this idea work? What are the benefits of this concept? What solutions would this idea bring about?

Now turn your entire focus and apply an equal amount of time (three minutes) to listing as many negatives for the same concept. Remember to concentrate totally on only the minuses. With practice, you should be able to come up with a fairly balanced sheet. Doing so requires that temporary suspension of judgment and emotion, however. There will be plenty of time for emotion later on. The questions to be asking here are: What is bad about this idea? Why wouldn't it work? What can I see wrong with this idea? What problems would it cause? What would be some of the adverse reactions to the concept?

This deliberate focusing of our attention to both sides of the concept in question is the beginning of opening the parameters of perception. It is a deliberate attempt to see both sides of an issue, but the **PMI** offers another dimension usually omitted from the thinking process, and that is the "Interesting" side. This is the clue to really and truly widening the parameters of our perception. Here is how it works.

After doing the pluses and the minuses, we focus an equal amount of time and energy exploring other (interesting) possibilities that stem from the original idea or concept. The key questions to ask here are: What if we tried this ... instead of the original idea? Like, instead of buying a new car, maybe we could buy a motorcycle? Suppose we tried this or that? Maybe we should keep the car we have and get a used car? Maybe we don't need another car at all. What if we took the bus? It doesn't matter where you go in this Interesting section. This is the place to get as creative as you can be, the only rule being to suspend judgment and emotion. Get creative and go crazy! Maybe we could parachute to work, or how about teleportation?

The purpose of this third and most important area, is to get us thinking in terms in which we would not ordinarily think. It is tapping into the right side of the brain and playing with any concept that comes to mind. We are not committing to any course of action here, so it is totally safe to do so. And it is often in this third area, the Interesting, that new inventions and innovations are discovered. That is the power of the **PMI**. It gets us out of our normal thinking box, and opens our minds up to an infinity of options, opportunities and possibilities that we may not have thought of, or even considered, without it. It is a mind-expanding skill, serving to exercise the mental muscles and release the adrenalin of creative thought.

Example:

PMI Concept: Buying a new car.

Plus:

Love the smell of a new car

My old one is dying

Better mileage

Safer

Better sound system

Investment

It would better fit my image

It would make me happy

More comfortable

I could drive more

(The list would go on, until the time is up. But you get the idea. Remember, as soon as a thought comes to mind, write it down. Do not stop to judge or think about it further. You can always go back and sort through them later.)

Minus:

Too expensive

Monthly payments

Insurance

Old car still runs

Hard to decide which one

No place to garage it

Too many car-jackings

Depreciation

Would have to drive less due to having less cash (Note how we took a positive and turned it into a negative . . . that is allowed.)

Little trade-in value for old car

(Again, the list would continue to grow until the time runs out. Remember to go for quantity, not quality.)

So far, the **PMI** is not unlike brainstorming, except that it is totally and deliberately focused on one area at a time.

Interesting:

What if I bought a more modern used car?

I could get a motorcycle and keep the old car

Perhaps I could win a new car in a contest

Maybe I could get a boat instead

What if I leased a new car and kept the old one?

I could start my own used car lot

I could go to work for a dealership

Maybe I could take flying lessons

How about a gyrocopter?

Or an ultra light airplane

Notice how, as we progress down the interesting section we can begin to get away from the original concept…that is perfectly acceptable, sometimes even *desirable*. It is in this area that innovative and creative ideas originate. Go with it! Let your mind have fun and play freely!

So this is the first Lateral Thinking skill. It is called the **PMI** (Plus/Minus/Interesting). Now it is time to practice. Get out a note pad, pen and a time-keeping device. Here is your first PMI exercise. Remember to suspend judgment and emotion and go for quantity. Try and list as many items in each particular area as you can in the time allotted. For this first one, we will give you three minutes per section.

PMI #1: *Concept: I should change my job.*

Three minutes for ONLY the Plus factors. (List as many as you possibly can.)

Three minutes for the Minus factors. (Remember to totally focus only on this area.)

Three minutes for the Interesting factors. (Wherever your thoughts lead you.)

The **PMI** is great for making decisions, solving problems, resolving differences and conflicts, planning, exploring new ideas, just about anything. As you practice, cut the time down to two minutes per section, then to a minute per section. You will find that your output will actually increase with practice, even though the time factor is less.

The **PMI** is also a great tool for groups, teams, couples and departments.

Simply have one person track the time, and another write down the ideas as people in the group shout them out. You will discover that the output will at least double as you begin to include the perceptions of others. Often someone will mention an idea you would never have thought of, which gets you thinking in an entirely different direction. This is, to me, one of the greatest benefits of group *PMI's*. You begin to realize the value and benefit of including the perceptions of others (different than your own), rather than the traditional approach of judging the ideas of other people as being "right" or "wrong" in relation to your own.

One great benefit I have found with the *PMI* is that it begins to open our own perception parameters. It gets us thinking creatively. I can't think of any occasion in which I have been working with a group of people doing *PMI's* that wasn't fun! And some of the ideas generated were worthy of further exploration. Some have turned into inventions and taken people in directions they wouldn't have dreamed of trying in a million years.

As you become more and more proficient, you will find that your mind will automatically perform instant *PMI's* as you are confronted with decisions and problems, and you will explore many different options before committing to any one of them . . . all in a split second.

But the greatest benefit of all, and do not miss the importance of this statement, is that it helps us to learn how to temporarily suspend our emotion and judgment. That, in and of itself, is worth its weight in gold!

Let's try another one.

PMI #2: Concept: *I should go back to / stay in school.*

Take three minutes for each area. Notice how the closer we get to one's core values and belief system, the more difficult it is to suspend emotion and judgement. For example, if we were to do a group PMI on an issue such as abortion, you would see some people finding it really difficult not to get emotionally involved. That is why you begin to learn these skills by practicing with fairly non-emotional issues, gradually building up your ability to suspend emotion and judgment, before tackling the larger issues. When performing the *PMI* with another person(s), remember not to judge each other's ideas. Just write them down. One person's Plus could be another person's Minus, or could be another person's Interesting.

Assignment

I want you to practice the **PMI** by coming up with three separate concepts to "play" with. Start with three minutes per section for the first one, two minutes for each section of the second PMI, and one minute per section for the third.

Then you are to select another human being (preferably one who is alive, breathing and capable of participating) and teach them this skill.

Finally, you are to practice at least three **PMI's** with that person or persons. The more you practice, the better you will become and the easier the skill will be to perform. Remember to have fun with this. The purpose is not to arrive at some earth-shattering conclusions, although that may happen in the process; the purpose is to expand the parameters of your perception, to exercise the mental muscles, to explore the creative side of your brain.

If you have difficulty at first, don't give up. Remember the first time you got on a bicycle and tried to solo? The same is true of these skills. Practice makes perfect. Also remember that this is a little contrary to the traditional thinking systems that we have been taught, so it may feel a little uncomfortable at first. So don't be deterred. Have fun with it.

You may even find, with any of these skills, that after completing the exercise, you come back to your original opinion. Was it a waste of time? Absolutely not! By applying these skills, you are surer than ever that your thinking is straight. You can rest assured that you have done your homework. Your can proceed with the assurance and confidence that you have applied the best thinking to the issue and that you aren't acting on a whim. So they can serve as reinforcing agents, as well as means for innovation.

Personal Action Plan

As I mentioned, there are three parts to the Personal Action Plan:

Part One: *Insights*

Take a few moments of silence and just think about this skill. What interesting insights did you gain? What possibilities do you see to use it? What benefits of the PMI do you see? Write them down.

Part Two: *Action*

Select a specific problem, decision, or concept, and commit to applying the PMI to it at a specific time, date, place, etc. The more specific you are, the better chance there is that you will fulfill your commitment to yourself. If you have performed the previous exercises, you should be ready to tackle a more perplexing or pressing problem, concept or issue.

Part Three: *Sharing*

Select one or more persons with whom you will share the PMI skill. You will teach it to them and actually do at least one with them. Again, be as specific as possible.

As we progress through the other skills, you should design and implement a Personal Action Plan for each. This is an extremely important part of the learning process. There are many reasons for the Personal Action Plan, most of which we have already discussed.

Consider All Factors (CAF)

Now for your second Lateral Thinking skill, the **CAF** (Consider All Factors)

Sometimes, when faced with a decision or in planning, we consider some factors, but not as many as we should. The **CAF** is a deliberate attempt to increase the number of factors we consider before committing to this course of action or that. It is not unlike brainstorming. It is less focused than the PMI.

Remember the Law of Requisite Variety? For those who have forgotten (none of you, I'm sure), it says that the more choices you have available to you, the more likely you are to make a better decision. The same goes for factors when you are considering making that decision. In the chapter regarding perceptions in Core Concepts, we looked at how our perceptions can be broadened simply by taking on board more information, right? Well, the **CAF** is the type of tool that guides you into collecting more of that information and by following the **CAF** system you will always consider more factors in the decision than had you not used it, thereby increasing the chances of making a better decision. This is a fundamental point we must embrace if we are going to improve the quality of our decisions and consequently the decisions we make in life. If we are to ensure that we do make better decisions, we must have quality information prior to the decision being made. When we receive quality information only *after* we have made a decision, our decision is far more likely to have been a mistake. Do you see the connection?

Let's look at an example of how the **CAF** works:

A couple is considering buying that new car. They have done a PMI on it, and have agreed that is what they are going to do. However, as yet they haven't learned the CAF skill. The following are the only factors they have considered up to this point:

Cost

Financing

Color

Make

Model

Dealership

Trade-in value of their old car

Resale value

What factors have they left out? How many more factors can you add? Let's try adding a few.

Air bags

Anti-skid braking system

Stereo system

Air conditioning

Convertible or hard top

Ash trays

Coffee holders (An important one for me! Whoops . . .sorry about that!)

Theft rate

Security system

Lo-jack

Insurance premiums increase?

Leasing versus buying

See what I mean? Any one of those factors could be a key element in making a "better" decision. By deliberately considering as many factors as possible, we are increasing our chances of making a choice that will be better. That is the importance of performing a **CAF**. It should be immediately obvious that it would be beneficial to include as many different perceptions as possible simply to increase the number of factors we consider. After all, our heart may be set on that pink convertible but if we consider the kids, the shopping the fuel economy and the fact that you are a Supreme Court Judge, suddenly we can see how certain factors can have a strong influence on what we *want* and assist us with making the decision based on what we really *need*.

Again, I want to point out that these skills lead us to appreciating the differences between *our own* perception, experiences and concepts, and those of others, rather than looking at those differences as barriers between ourselves and others. They are "inclusive" by their nature, rather than exclusive.

Time for you to do a **CAF**. But be careful. Remember that the Law of Requisite Variety puts value on the *number* of choices, not the *quality*! In the stages before making a decision, *quantity* is important, not *quality*. We will have plenty of time later to consider whether any given factor is important enough to include in your final decision. Don't censor your thoughts when writing down the factors, just concentrate your mind on getting as many as you can, as quickly as you can. If you're practicing this in a group this is particularly important. Don't censor other's thoughts; don't even discuss them at this point. Just let them all stream forth and use the limited time you have wisely to get as many factors as is humanly possible.

Right then, let's go for it!

CAF Concept #1: *Buying a house*

See how many factors involved in buying a house you can list in three minutes. Remember to go for quantity. That is the key to a successful CAF.

CAF Concept #2: *Choosing a career*

Only two minutes this time. See how many factors are involved here.

As you can see, when we are performing a *CAF*, we are not concerned with pluses or minuses. We are not categorizing the factors, simply listing as many as we can. There is always time to go back later and sort through them.

How many times have we said, in retrospect, "Oh if only I had considered that?" or "I wish I hadn't said that! Why didn't I think before opening my big mouth and inserting both feet?" The *CAF* will help us to avoid, or at least

diminish, the number of times we regret making foolish statements, decisions, or acting in a non-thinking manner we will later regret. It allows us to consider as many factors as possible before committing to a particular course of action, and therein is the power of the *CAF*.

Assignment

Now I would like you to do three more *CAF*'s, starting with three minutes for the first, two for the second, and one minute for the third. Pick any concept. It's your option. Maybe it is about getting married, or deals with changing jobs, or continuing your education. The concept you are dealing with for the purposes of practice is not as important as simply doing them.

CAF Personal Action Plan

Now that you know how to perform the *CAF*, it is time for a Personal Action Plan. In this respect, the Personal Action Plan for the *CAF* is the same as the PMI.

Insights

Performing a Specific CAF

Sharing

The OPV (Other People's Views)

The final Lateral Thinking skill I am going to present to you here is called the **OPV** (Other People's Views). I would hope by now, if you have been doing your assignments and carrying through with your Personal Action Plans that you have begun to accept the fact that other people think differently than you do. I would also hope that you are beginning to see the value of including other points of view with your own. Can you see how doing so increases and expands your own perception? This is really the basis for synergy (the power of a system being greater than the sum of all its individual parts). In fact, it is one of the basic elements of synergy.

The **OPV** is a deliberate stepping out of our own thinking and "walking for a few minutes in the other person's shoes." It is a deliberate attempt to view the situation, concept, or problem from their perception, not our own. What is the value here? For one thing, it helps us to become more tolerant of the ideas of others. It also enables us to become more pro-active listeners and it increases our levels of sensitivity and awareness.

The **OPV** could be one of the greatest tools I have ever discovered to place our own egos on hold and consider others and their feelings in the decision making process. It is great for negotiating, avoiding and resolving conflicts, planning, and just about any other activity that involves other people. That includes the "personal" decisions we make.

Remember the pebble in the pond and the impact, both direct and indirect, that our decisions and choices have on others? Well, the OPV is designed to take those ripples into consideration *before* committing to a course of action that is going to affect other people.

Let's look at an example.

A couple is considering marriage. Take three minutes for each and do an OPV on what they might be thinking. The key to performing a successful OPV is to actually make yourself *become* the other person. *Make all statements as if you were actually he or she.*

He:

I am concerned about being able to support a family

I am a little nervous about making a life-time commitment

I really love her

The sex is great

She really understands me

I think she loves me

She would make a great mother

She would be a wonderful partner

I am not sure I am mature enough for the increased responsibility

She:

I know I love him

He tends to look at other women

My own parents divorced and that makes me a little nervous

I want to pursue my own career

I am not sure I am ready for motherhood

We would both have to work to support us

Maybe we should wait a year and put some money aside

I'd like a big wedding

We seem to argue a lot

The sex is adequate

I think he is the person I want to spend the rest of my life with

As you can see, there are many differences . . . and similarities here. Let's delve into the OPV just a little deeper. The purpose of the **OPV** is not to get inside the other person's head so that you can manipulate that person. That would be a violation of principle. The purpose is to *increase our own level of sensitivity*. This is a key issue.

Does it matter whether or not you correctly identify all the thoughts of the other person? No. What matters is that you are making the attempt to understand the situation from the other person's point of view. It makes us much more cognizant of the feelings of others, and this can be of great value in dealing with others.

The OPV can be a wonderful tool in preparing for a negotiating session.

Let's use such an example as our first practice.

***OPV* #1**: *Asking your boss for a raise*

Do a three-minute OPV on your boss.

***OPV* #2**: *Trouble at Work*

You are a supervisor. Lately, you have noticed a rising tension between one of your male employees and one of your female employees. Do a two-minute OPV on each.

Can you see the value in taking a moment to consider the situation from the standpoint of the other people involved? I was once conducting training for a company in which there was a married couple participating in separate sessions. (I was doing three per day due to the large number of people involved.) I taught Lateral Thinking one week and the following week, the people returned to share the results of their assignments.

In the morning session, the husband, who had not actively volunteered to share in any previous sessions, immediately jumped in and told us that he was totally amazed at what he had experienced with the ***OPV*** and his wife. The following is the story, as he related it:

"My wife and I, the other night, got into what you refer to as a "difference of opinion," and I don't know where the idea came from, but I suggested we each do an OPV on the other, to which she agreed. So we sat down and I wrote out what I thought she was thinking and she did the same about what she thought I was thinking. At the end, we exchanged papers and read them.

"I looked up in astonishment and said, 'Wait a minute! This is not where I am coming from at all!' She replied that my impressions of her thinking were all wrong, as well. We then put down the papers and began to talk about our true feelings. Now, our normal approach is to go into two or three days without speaking at all, and this approach enabled us to reach a resolution within a half hour or so. It was the first time that has ever happened!"

He was truly excited. I couldn't wait to hear her side of the story. When the afternoon session rolled around, sure enough, when I asked for people to share their assignment results, she willingly told practically the same version. What had changed here? The only thing that had changed was that they had found a tool that enabled them to communicate, rather than shutting down, as had been their modus operandi for years. Therein lies the power of the

OPV.

In terms of negotiating, the OPV has value by enabling us to envision possible objections and prepare ourselves for them in advance. I have often used the OPV in such circumstances successfully.

Another area in which I have found the *OPV* to be of great value is in the area of customer service. As the supervisor on airplanes for so many years, I was the person who had to deal with people's problems while locked up with them in an aluminum tube at 35,000 feet. There was no other place to go! As the person or persons would be relating their problem to me, I would be making a deliberate attempt to see the problem from their point of view. As a result, I was much more effective at helping them than if I had been trying to defend myself or the airlines against a perceived attack!

Assignment

I want you to perform *three OPV's* on personal situations involving other people. Remember to include *all* persons involved, directly and indirectly. Also remember to make a deliberate attempt to actually become that other person and see the situation through their eyes.

Personal Action Plan

You know the drill by now. Go out there and do it.

Summary

The three Lateral Thinking skills I have presented here are the most powerful skills I have ever encountered. I remember, when I first learned them, the first people I shared them with were my wife and son. He was eight years old at the time. Now he's thirty and, to this day, we still apply them individually and as a family.

You can use these three skills independent of one another. You can apply all three to the same situation or concept. You can do a CAF first, then a PMI on just one of the factors. You can do a *CAF* on an Interesting idea from a PMI. They are all interconnected and, when used as a system, they will increase your thinking power tremendously. You will become a more sensitive and aware thinker. Your thinking process will be more inclusive and complete. You will become a better problem solver, decision maker, conflict resolver and planner.

Conclusions

I sincerely believe that, by becoming a better thinker, you increase your own potential and, by expanding your perception, you proportionately increase the number of opportunities you will be able to perceive and create for yourself in life. Better thinkers are what we need. These are skills that are universally applicable. You will carry them and the power they provide with you the rest of your life. Finally, they will increase the quality of your life, since everything we say and do begins with a thought.

Use them and practice them as often as you can. You will reach a point at which they are second nature to you. I remember one manager standing up and objecting that he just didn't have the time to apply these skills. My reply was that, with practice, we are talking about mere seconds, then asking him if he could really afford not to become a better thinker. Still, I pointed out, it was his choice.

As I mentioned at the beginning of this chapter, there are over a hundred Lateral Thinking skills developed by Edward de Bono, each with a specific purpose. Taken together, they represent a powerful thinking system that cannot help but add quality to your life decisions. I highly recommend his approach. It literally changed my life.

As we continue through the other steps, I will be suggesting that you apply these skills periodically, both for practice and because they work so well at sorting out our thoughts and examining new concepts, as well as old.

Speaking of old and new concepts, these skills are also very useful when it comes time to sort through assumptions on which we base our belief systems. That is something we will be doing in the chapter dealing with principles.

The addition of Lateral Thinking to our traditional system of linear logic is fundamental in forming the basis for an unbeatable thinking system that is both logical and creative, sensible and innovative. No matter what company, group, organization or individual, with which I have consulted, Lateral Thinking has always been, by far, the biggest hit.

ABOUT THE AUTHOR

Terry Jackson is a highly accomplished, experienced and dynamic Executive Advisor, Thought Leader, and Organizational Consultant. Terry is a Coach and Consultant for US State Department International Information Program and the Duke University Executive Education Program . Terry's passion and purpose is helping others improve their quality of life and achieve performance excellence.

Terry is a visionary with 25+ years of progressive leadership experience in sales, marketing, operations management, and business consulting within startups and Fortune 10 companies. Terry holds a Ph.D. in Leadership and Organizational Change. Terry is an authority in Diversity in Business, Emotional Intelligence and its use to create high levels of employee engagement and sustained performance.

Terry has demonstrated success in catapulting sales, expanding existing markets, building strategic business relationships, and developing professionals. Terry has extensive experience in P&L management, new product launches, corporate turnarounds, brand management, contract negotiations, auditing, people development, and several process improvement methodologies.

Terry has worked with and consulted for companies such giants as Norfolk Southern Corp, ExxonMobil, Bristol Meyers Squibb, New York Life, Valassis, Dell-EMC, PioneerSol, Bahria University, Lahore University of Management Science, NED University, National Incubation Center, HIVE, KITE Incubator, and FedEx. Terry is currently engaged with the Pakistan government on several major consulting projects.

Terry has led large scale consulting and coaching engagements in the following industries: Education, Financial, Petroleum, Telecommunications, State and Federal Government, Retail and Consumer Package Goods